The Spiritual Journey
of Jimmy Carter

The Spiritual Journey of Jimmy Carter

IN HIS OWN WORDS

COMPILED, AND WITH AN INTRODUCTION BY
WESLEY G. PIPPERT

Macmillan Publishing Co., Inc.
NEW YORK

Collier Macmillan Publishers
LONDON

Macmillan Publishing Co., Inc.
866 Third Avenue, New York, N.Y. 10022
Collier Macmillan Canada, Ltd.

Library of Congress Cataloging in Publication Data

Carter, Jimmy, 1924–
    The spiritual journey of Jimmy Carter, in his
own words.

    1. Carter, Jimmy, 1924–   —Religion.
2. Presidents—United States—Biography.
I. Pippert, Wesley. II. Title.
E873.2.C38   248.2′092′4 [B]   78-16324
ISBN 0-02-597590-0

First Printing 1978

Printed in the United States of America

Permission is gratefully acknowledged for use of various selections from other
publications:

Excerpts from Jimmy Carter, *Why Not the Best?* (Nashville: Broadman Press
1975). Used by permission.

Excerpts from an interview by Bill Moyers, "USA: People and Politics, A Conversation with Jimmy Carter," co-produced by WNET/Thirteen, New York,
and WETA/26, Washington, D.C., May 6, 1976. Reprinted by permission.

Excerpts from an interview with Jimmy Carter by Ralph Blodgett published by
Liberty magazine, September–October, 1976. Used by permission of *Liberty* magazine, Washington, D.C.

Excerpts from an interview with Jimmy Carter by Jim Castelli, Washington,
D.C., August 9, 1976. Copyright 1976 by the National Catholic News Service.

Response by Jimmy Carter to a question asked by Cal Thomas of KPRC-TV
News, Houston, Texas, April 20, 1976.

An excerpt from an interview with Jimmy Carter by James Reston on December
1, 1977, published in *The New York Times*, December 5, 1977. © by The New
York Times Company. Reprinted by permission.

Excerpts from an interview with Jimmy Carter by Robert Scheer, November
1976. Copyright © 1976 by Playboy.

Excerpts from an interview with Jimmy Carter during the 1976 campaign by Pat
Robertson, Christian Broadcasting Network.

To Mother,
who prays for Jimmy Carter daily
as she does for me

Contents

Contents

[x]

Contents

III. RELIGION AND POLITICS

Contents

Preface

THE PREPARATION OF THIS BOOK grew out of my own conviction that Jimmy Carter's belief in Christ and perhaps his very essence were not being communicated clearly or competently to the American people.

I was assigned to the Carter campaign by United Press International in June 1976 shortly after he had been assured of the Democratic presidential nomination. As with many politicians, we reporters tended to view Carter, by and large, in typical political ways. Yet this seemed inadequate in defining him. His faith and his explicit expression of it probably were novel for most politicians and for most reporters. I am not at all certain we succeeded either for ourselves or our audiences in learning and communicating the essence of the man who became president.

I have tried to assemble every statement of a religious nature that Carter made publicly during the final six months of his campaign and the first year and a half of his administration. Many of them I myself heard. Some of them have been published previously, but many of them have not. Taken as a whole, I think they go far in getting at the core of Jimmy Carter's life.

Some of the prayers and Sunday-school lessons were tape-recorded. For the other prayers and lessons used here, I have detailed notes, often compared and checked carefully with other reporters. I am indebted to many colleagues for texts of their own interviews with Carter.

In this book, I have presented Carter's words exactly as he said them, except for minor grammatical corrections or deletions of such words as "well" and "you know." Any omissions of substance are indicated by an ellipsis. Nothing of consequence has been omitted. I have omitted, primarily, remarks such as introductory comments to a speech or repetitious or partial sentences. Where repetitions remain, as, for example, on the sin of pride or on the habit of prayer, I have retained them because they seemed to me to add another dimension to understanding Carter's thought. I have made the style of punctuation and capitalization consistent throughout. The headings are excerpted or adapted from the individual selections.

Carter usually uses the King James version of the Bible, and that is the version used in this book unless otherwise indicated. Biblical and other references in brackets are my insertions. The scripture index shows how deeply he is steeped in the Bible.

I also testify that this book grew out of my own sense of spiritual kinship with Jimmy Carter (a kinship, by the way, that I have never discussed with him). I, too, accepted Jesus Christ as my Saviour as a boy, only I did it at my mother's knee. Her predawn prayers sustain me to this day. I, too, was nurtured by parents who exemplified in their personal lives and in concern for their neighbors the

love and lordship of Christ. I have never escaped the
Hound of Heaven. I have come to see that God, through
Christ, seeks to redeem institutions and governments as
well as persons, changes that take place sometimes in orderly ways, sometimes through upheaval.

So this book really had its beginnings on an Iowa farm
in a family tightly welded by love. And it, and I, have
been shaped by certain others. They know who they are
and that they have my enduring love.

My list of acknowledgments is long.

I especially thank Helen Thomas, my colleague, the
best reporter in the White House, the person who made
this book happen, and most of all, a person who deeply
cares. I also thank my colleague Larry McQuillan, always
helpful, and Grant Dillman, the UPI Washington manager and a journalist of skill and vision. It was he who told
me: "We must define Jimmy Carter to the American people."

I also thank Kandy Stroud, herself author of an ex-
cellent book on the Carter campaign, for her help on the
prayers and lessons of the summer of 1976; John Hart of
NBC, who understands what Carter is about; Jody Powell
and his White House press staff; Rick Meyer of the Associated Press, and Pam Reeves of UPI for their help on
certain lessons; Suzanne Wiggins and Barry Garrett, two
helpful Southern Baptists; John Novotney, of Religious
News Service; Cal Thomas, of International Media Services; Pat Robertson, of the Christian Broadcasting Network; Harold Best, dean of music at Wheaton College,
and Jim Wall, Carter's 1976 Illinois chairman and editor of
Christian Century, with whom I have had my most in-
sightful conversations about Carter; and Paul Henry, a

political scientist who helped me with criticism of my introduction, and better yet, a close friend.

I am deeply grateful to Bill Griffin of Macmillan, and to Jeannette Hopkins, an editor whose work is as esthetic as it is skillful. I respect her profoundly. I am very grateful to Sheila Bell, a typist of competence and calm; to Ace Fleming and Ed Bradley of CBS, who helped when it really mattered; and to those who helped locate Carter's quotations: Jim McGraw; Dave Gilson, Catholic University theological librarian; and Myron M. Weinstein, Library of Congress Hebraic specialist.

And, especially, to Becky. We both know why.

WES PIPPERT
Washington, D.C.
February 1978

Introduction: Jimmy Carter's Spiritual Biography

1. A Life Is Changed

"You took us in, you've given us stability in a position that is inherently sometimes unstable, and you've given us a sense of belonging. Quite often a president of our great country can be isolated from the surrounding world. Whether you're a lonesome farm boy in Plains, Georgia, fifty years ago, or in the White House now reaching out for human understanding across the ocean, or a candidate looking for a common ground to understand one another, the thing that ties them together is a common belief in Christ."

Jimmy Carter was speaking at a church supper at the thirty-third annual banquet of the couples' class at the First Baptist Church eight blocks from the White House. When it was his turn to speak, he talked about his boyhood near Plains, Georgia, about gathering a handful of smooth, flat rocks from the railroad bed. He had hated to throw them away when his mother called him to the house for some freshly baked cookies. The story, he said, symbolized the kind of decision he often faces as president and that others face in their personal lives—how to drop what we have at hand, which seems important, in order to accept the free gift of love from God. In this modern world, he said, we tend to get away from clinging to things that are important. He thanked the class for welcoming him and his family.

Jody Powell, who has been Jimmy Carter's chief interpreter to the public since 1970, has said that the American people, on the whole, are better equipped to understand the spiritual aspects of Carter's life than "the people who are trying to explain it to them." In other words, that we in the press, among others, have seriously misunderstood Carter's faith in Christ and have, therefore, portrayed him erroneously or as an enigma.

A Washington lawyer told me in Plains during the summer of 1976 that she thought fundamentalism implied Holy Rollers and snake handlers and a presumptuous "pipeline to God" attitude. Her attitude was typical. When, during the 1976 North Carolina primary, Carter's "born again" experience first received wide attention, a network anchorman remarked, "incidentally, we've checked this out. Being 'born again' is not a bizarre experience or the voice of God from the mountaintop. It's a fairly common experience known to millions of Americans—particularly if you're Baptist." Another network anchorman asked Carter a few months later whether his evangelical Christianity would cause him to "demand Baptist standards of behavior and morals from everybody else." Such remarks suggest a fundamental lack of understanding of the Christian faith and, therefore, of Jimmy Carter himself.

There is frequently an attitude of cynicism among the news media toward politicians who profess faith. As a consequence, while reporters may ask pointed questions about belief during a campaign, newspaper and television coverage of belief as a key to understanding of the person is sporadic, superficial, fragmented, and often out of context. We compound the problem of public understanding of the candidate and the President. Yet when Carter spoke to a forum of high-school students in Nashua, New Hampshire, in February 1978, a number of the young questioners asked him about his faith and its significance to him as president. Did he believe that he should repent for the nation? Did he have a responsibility to uphold moral standards? The nation's press gave his answers only glancing attention. The president had made no "news" (but perhaps he had offered an incisive glimpse of himself).

This episode symbolizes faith in Jesus Christ that is the motive power of Jimmy Carter's life, the longing for what endures in times of change and instability, the conviction that God's grace and love are available to all who will accept it, and that Christ is the living Son of God.

Many persons have equated Carter's religious views exclusively with the "Bible belt" or the rural South. They identified being "born again" as distinctively Baptist. But the experience of conversion, "being saved" or "born again," is common to many in big cities, small towns, and rural areas throughout the world. There are persons who profess to be "born again" in the fundamentalist and evangelical denominations as well as in main-line Protestant denominations and the Roman Catholic Church. The experience is not unique to any denomination, to any group, to any area. It is a biblical experience.

Carter is, in New Testament language, "a believer" in Christ. Christ, to him, is God made manifest in the world.

Jimmy Carter has been a believer in Jesus Christ since childhood. The Baptist church always has been at the core of his daily living. He was raised steeped in the Bible—the first verse he learned, as a boy of four, was I John 4:8, "God is love." And devotion to the concept of love dominates his expression today. In his hometown of Plains, an isolated rural community, Carter felt assurance and warmth and security. "We felt close to nature, close to the members of our family, and close to God," he said of his early years in his autobiography, *Why Not the Best?*

Carter has told the story of his spiritual journey many times. He accepted Christ as his Saviour at eleven, was baptized in the Plains Baptist Church, taught Sunday school at the U.S. Naval Academy to children of enlisted men and officers stationed in Annapolis. On board ship and submarines, he conducted worship services for crewmen on special days. After his father's death, when he resigned from the Navy to run the family's peanut business, he plunged back into the life of the Plains church. He volunteered to become a Sunday-school teacher, served as superintendent of the junior-high division, as a deacon—an important leadership role in Baptist churches—and chairman of the deacons, and, later, as head of the brotherhood commission for thirty-four Southern Baptist churches in Georgia.

One day Carter told his pastor during revival services that he was considering running for the Georgia Senate. If he really wanted to be of service to other people, he should go into the ministry or social-service work, the pastor advised. But to Carter, politics was a ministry, and the voters a congregation. As he tells it, he answered, "How would you like to be the pastor of a church with eighty thousand members?"

Carter ran for the state senate, won, and in 1966 aimed for and lost the governor's chair, defeated by Lester Maddox. In those days, failure was a traumatic experience for him. His faith did not sustain him and he soon experienced a spiritual crisis. He began to ponder the depth of his conviction.

"I was very proud of my status in the church," he has said. "Then I began to realize that the personal relationship between me and Christ was not very significant in my life."

As he writes in his autobiography, he computed that he had visited 140 families for the church in the fourteen years he had been home from the navy. He was proud of his record, but then he realized that, in the search of votes during his unsuccessful campaign for governor, he had reached 300,000 persons—300,000 for politics but only 140 visits for God.

Searching in the Bible for guidance, he read in Luke 18:10–14 about the Pharisees, the churchmen of Jesus' day, who took great pride and satisfaction in the fact that they were not extortioners, adulterers, or tax collectors like other men. Jesus told them that he that humbleth himself shall be exalted. This is the Bible story Carter refers to perhaps more frequently than any other.

"For the first time I saw that *I* was the Pharisee," he said.

He was influenced also by a sermon of which he remembers only the title, "If you were arrested for being a Christian, would there be enough evidence to convict you?"

"And my answer by the time that sermon was over was 'No'," Carter said in an interview with Bill Moyers of the Public Broadcasting Service on May 6, 1976. "I never had really committed myself totally to God—my Christian beliefs were superficial. Based primarily on pride and—I'd never done much for other people. I was always thinking about myself, and I changed somewhat for the better. I formed a much more intimate relationship with Christ. And, since then, I've had just about like a new life."

He became a missionary for a short period, visiting families to witness to them about Christ. At first he spurned an invitation to go. He thought and prayed about it. It occurred to him that he had never given one hour of his life to God with absolutely no strings attached. He would give time to God and go. In Massachusetts, where he witnessed, in company with Eloy Cruz, a Cuban pastor to the Spanish-speaking people, forty-six people accepted Christ as their Saviour during one week. The witnessing mission touched his life. Later, during his long presidential campaign, he never showed deep emotion, never cried, but he said that when he and Cruz parted that week tears were running down his own cheeks.

In 1968 he was one of six Southern Baptist laymen who went to Lock Haven, Pennsylvania, to "bear witness." "I realized very quickly I didn't have much testimony to give. I really didn't know God. . . . I had no intimate relationship with Christ," he told the men's Bible class at the Plains Baptist Church on December 12, 1976. After he was elected governor in his second try he wrote a letter to Mr. and Mrs. Robert Farwell of Lock Haven that in their community he had been "closest to Christ and first experienced in a personal and intense way the presence of the Holy Spirit in my life" (1976 Associated Press dispatch).

Carter has frequently testified that these witnessing missions brought him closer to the Holy Spirit. Through these missions he had begun to feel "personally present to the Holy Spirit" and able to testify for the first time with complete sincerity about what Christ meant to me. I found it easy to pray without a special extra effort; it became part of my consciousness, and I felt a sense of peace and security that I had never felt before. I felt that Christ was a constant part of my daily life and recognized much more clearly my own failures, fallibilities, and sinfulness. I didn't feel embarrassed when I prayed about them. I was able to face them in a lot more relaxed and perhaps more courageous way, and without reticence. I felt that when I asked God for forgiveness it was there. . . .

"The intimacy with which I have accepted Christ in my own heart and the realization of the presence of the Holy Spirit, of my own need and how my need can be filled by Christ, the fact that I'm not better than other people but just have received the special blessing of God because He loves me through Jesus Christ, those personal realizations came much more forcefully to me later on in my life."

His sister, Ruth Carter Stapleton, who is a charismatic evangelist, described her brother's experience after his defeat for office in 1966. "He was a 'church Christian.' . . . Jimmy was having a series of awarenesses of some lacks in his life, maybe motivation, a sense of direction. It was a time of self-analysis. . . .

"He already had had two or three religious experiences. But he was wondering whether he was doing enough, caring enough for mankind. Then he moved into a new dimension . . . a deeper commitment. I don't know that he had ever made a complete commitment of his political life before. After that, Christ came first because his ambitions were very fervent at the time. So it was a whole new phase of life that he was moving into. It was to serve Christ in his work."

Carter continued to be active in the Baptist church, in Atlanta as governor and in Plains as a presidential candidate. He taught Sunday school in Plains about once a month. In 1976, after he won the Iowa caucus in January and the New Hampshire primary in March, more and more people became aware of his personal faith. ABC's Sam Donaldson recalls that Carter dodged reporters' questions about it for several days. Then, on March 18, 1976, during the North Carolina primary campaign, he addressed it fully in public for the first time.

"I spent more time on my knees the four years I was governor in the seclusion of a little private room off the governor's office," Carter told his audience of contributors in Winston-Salem, "than I did in all the rest of my life put together because I felt so heavily on my shoulders the decisions I made might very well affect many, many people.

"I recognized for the first time that I had lacked something very precious—a complete commitment to Christ, a presence of the Holy Spirit in my life in a more profound and personal way. And since then I've had an inner peace and inner conviction and assurance that transformed my life for the better. . . ."

The next day, he was questioned at a news conference.

"In 1967, I realized my own relationship with God was a very superficial one. . . . I began to realize that my Christian life, which I had always professed to be preeminent, had really been a secondary interest in my life, and I formed a very close, personal, intimate relationship with God through Christ that has given me a great deal of peace, equanimity. . . .

"It was not a profound stroke, a miracle, a voice of God from heaven. It was not anything of that kind. It wasn't anything mysterious. It was the same kind of experience that many have who become Christians in a deeply personal way and it has given me a deep feeling of equanimity and peace."

As president, Carter has continued to teach Sunday school, although now it is the couples' class at the First Baptist Church in Washington, D.C. He is, as he put it, "a part-time substitute teacher." The style of his teaching and the biblical content of the lessons have not varied from Plains to Washington. His public statements and speeches as president only rarely carry any direct reference to his faith, though he answers questions when put to him about it. It is his prayers and talks in Sunday school that have provided the real insight, in this reporter's view, into Jimmy Carter the man and the president. It is part of his witnessing.

2. *Interpreting Carter's Faith*

"Born again," "saved," "converted," "justified," "redeemed"—all are biblical in origin and usage, used by Jesus and the biblical writers in describing in limited, human ways the miraculous change that may transform a person who believes in Jesus Christ as Lord and Saviour. Terms such as "born again" have become clichés and stripped of meaning. But each has a precise meaning.

"Believe" means more than mere intellectual assent ("For God so loved the world, that he gave his only begotten Son, that whosoever believeth in him should not perish, but have everlasting life"—John 3:16). "Born again" or "reborn" or "twice-born" means to emerge from darkness into a new life of the spirit ("Except a man be born again, he cannot see the kingdom of God"—John 3:3). "Saved" suggests life-and-death implications ("He that believeth and is baptized shall be saved; but he that believeth not shall be damned"—Mark 16:16). "Converted" means to turn about ("Except ye be converted, and become as little children, ye shall not enter into the kingdom of heaven"—Matthew 18:3). "Justified" has the legal implications of justice (Jesus "was delivered for our offences, and was raised again for our justification"—Romans 4:25). "Redeemed" has commercial implications (". . . ye know that ye were not redeemed with corruptible things, *as* silver and gold . . . but with the precious blood of Christ"—I Peter 1:18–19). "Commitment" implies a vow or promise (Paul said he was persuaded that Jesus Christ "is able to keep that which I have committed unto him against that day"—II Timothy 1:12).

Fundamentalism represents the historical tenets of the Christian faith. The term grew out of the vigorous debate in the early 1900s in the United States over humanism and liberalism and "modernism." These five points emerged as "fundamental" to the faith: the virgin birth of Jesus Christ, His physical resurrection, the infallibility of the Bible, the substitutionary atonement by Christ on the cross, and the physical second coming of Christ. Those points constitute pure fundamentalism; thus Carter is a fundamentalist. However, he does not fit the stereotype of the fundamentalist who is often judgmental, often preoccupied with hell or heaven.

Carter believes in spiritual discipline. He and his wife read the Bible together nightly. He prays frequently during the day—"almost like breathing," he remarked to this reporter, "not often in a structured way but asking God for wisdom or sound judgment or compatibility with people who depend upon me. . . ." A well-worn King James version of the Bible lies on his desk in the Oval Office. He observes a strict moral code in his personal behavior. The Carters stopped the serving of hard liquor at White House social events, and he is, for all practical purposes, a teetotaler. He says he has never smoked a cigarette in his life. He says he has loved one woman in his life and he is married to her; their shared faith has sustained their marriage (interview by Robert Scheer, *Playboy*, November 1976). A strict adherent of the Ten Commandments, he shows no hesitancy, however, in spending Sunday afternoon and evening in the White House—at work.

There are recurring themes in his prayers and teachings—that all persons have sinned, that because of this nobody is better in God's eyes than anyone else, that eternal life depends on faith in Jesus Christ and on God's grace, that belief is simple and childlike. His theology is Christ-centered. There can be no doubt of this. During the Middle East crisis he quoted Arab leaders as saying that Jews and Moslems are sons of Abraham. In that sense, which is biblically accurate, Jews, Christians, and Moslems do worship the same God. The crucial difference, of course, is that Carter unquestioningly accepts the divinity of Christ.

Carter also has a biblically precise understanding of the Holy Spirit as God's agent on earth, made manifest in a person's effectiveness and ecstasy, in work and worship. Carter's sister, Ruth Stapleton, participates in divine healings, speaks in tongues, and expresses other more dramatic "gifts of the spirit." There is no evidence that Carter himself speaks in tongues, but he frequently has said that the Holy Spirit is meaningful to him.

[11]

When Bill Moyers asked whether he had doubts about himself, about God, about life, Carter replied, "I can't think of any." He has no doubts about his own purpose and his faith, though he finds choices among policies no easy task. He acknowledged in an interview with Pat Robertson, a charismatic Christian and son of a U.S. senator, that reporters have often mistaken his inner peace for arrogance.

As president, Carter has been more forthrightly devout and articulate in his personal beliefs than any recent Chief Executive. "I do pray often and seek His guidance before I make any major decision," he said to a men's Sunday-school class at the Baptist church in Calhoun, Georgia, on Easter Sunday 1977. He told a group of Georgia campaign volunteers that he really needed their prayers. At the swearing-in ceremony for Paul C. Warnke, whose nomination as arms negotiator was one of the most controversial of his administration, he remarked that he had "thought and prayed a lot" about who should be named to the post.

He trusts in God's wisdom in his own victories and defeats, but he is clear about never asking God for victory. James M. Wall, his Illinois campaign chairman and editor of *Christian Century*, the preeminent liberal Protestant magazine, asked Carter how he responded to his defeat in the 1976 Massachusetts presidential primary. "Rosalynn and I discussed it a great deal," Wall said Carter replied. "And we finally concluded it was for the best." Wall said he knew it was "the statement of a man of faith who believes that God transforms all events, the good and the bad, if we are receptive to His grace."

There is a paradox in the Christian faith. It imparts both a feeling of abject humility and a feeling of serene confidence. Persons who follow Christ must be aware, acutely aware, of their unworthiness and sinfulness. They also have the balancing assurance that they have been forgiven and emancipated from the bondage of sin. They know joy. But joy and confidence can lead to pride. Pride has been a trial and temptation for Carter himself. He seeks humility, but the search has not dampened his self-confidence.

The media thus missed the point in Carter's controversial *Playboy* interview (November 1976) in which he said he had lusted in his heart. Reporters leaped on his confession and his earthy use of language. Actually, Carter was merely acknowledging what most have committed in their own hearts but do not acknowledge. Carter was making a biblically valid point about pride: He who hates is as guilty as the person who murders; to lust is as grievous as to commit adultery. No one, therefore, has a right to condemn anyone else. Let him who is without sin throw the first stone. If there is a hierarchy of sin in God's eyes, Carter said, the worst is pride: "What Christ taught about most was pride, that one person should never think he was any better than anybody else." He has repeated that admonition many times. Also, to Carter, the *Playboy* interview was an occasion of witnessing, perhaps similar to the missions in earlier days. A few days after the interview became almost notorious, he told reporters who were standing on the tarmac at the Houston airport that the *Playboy* audience hears far too little about Christian belief and moral standards. A short time later Carter met with AFL-CIO regional executives in the Northwest. "I don't have any apology to make for it," he told a questioner at the Portland session on September 27, 1976. "It was a good way to let the American people, particularly *Playboy* readers, know about my religious beliefs."

Introduction: Jimmy Carter's Spiritual Biography

The mass media generally have been less than competent or clear in dealing with the moral dimensions of a public issue or a politician. This was true in the coverage of George McGovern's 1972 presidential campaign. It was true during the Watergate crisis when the media, once awakened to the story, did a far better job of recounting the story of the White House tapes than in defining what there is about power that makes those who have it so vulnerable to using it. And it was true of coverage of Jimmy Carter. Months after he became president, stories still appeared about the mystery of the man. Meanwhile, few reporters bothered covering Carter at Sunday school, and few wire-service stories about his teaching got into print. Reporters have been confused because it was difficult for many to believe that religious faith could mold political philosophy. It is a serious omission, in this reporter's view, because his comments there may reveal who Jimmy Carter really is.

For Jimmy Carter's faith in Christ is manifested in his attitudes, motivations, ideals, anxieties, hopes, doubts, and intentions. Much that he says, of course, can be understood as reflecting his background of traditional Christianity, but much appears to be an expression of an intimate commitment to Christ. Consistent and constant themes emerge in his thought—not only doctrinal (for example, belief in the Second Coming of Christ) but personal.

The core of his religious and personal faith seems to be the core of his political philosophy as well. His central theme is that persons, and nations, are fallible and sinful and require forgiveness; that persons, and nations—perhaps especially the United States—are "afflicted," as he said *he* has been, by pride and need to learn humility; that persons and nations also have the capacity for goodness and that the same qualities that make for goodness in personal life—love, compassion, truth, justice, fidelity, patience, discipline, and so on—will make for goodness in public life. He is not an elitist—he believes some persons are stronger and some weaker but that none is better than others in the eyes of God. There should be a single standard, but if the laws of human beings violate the laws of God, Christians must obey God's laws and take the consequences by accepting civil punishment.

The personal emphasis on doing good, the reliance on private responsibility for good without leaving the entire burden to government, the trust in shared religious commitment among world leaders and personal negotiation as a basis for peace, particularly in the Middle East—all demonstrate the centrality of individuals to Carter and his understanding of government not as an impersonal institution but as a community of human beings. Trust, faith, love are necessary for good government. The strong are required to serve the weak and to minister to the suffering. On these matters, as on his faith, Carter has no doubts. It is about decisions among options of policy that he expresses doubt.

Carter shows great candor about his faith, though he is circumspect and reserved about his personal family life, and he is willing to make himself vulnerable to ridicule and misunderstanding as a witness to his faith. He has an absolute certitude about the rightness of his faith in Jesus Christ and about the presence of God and the truth of the Bible. This relationship of intimacy with Christ and the Holy Spirit gives him self-confidence and joy, equanimity, and inner peace. No longer, as in the past, he says, does he have a sense of separation from God or a fear of personal failure; victory or defeat are now accepted as the will of God. Death is not a threat but merely part of eternal life. He cherishes the prayers of the people and prays, in turn, that he will not "disappoint" them. But to him the relationship with Christ requires constant searching; he is not content, though stability and confidence in what does not change is essential to him. He speaks of stretching one's heart.

He accepts the Bible and the truth of the teachings of Jesus *a priori*, without questioning. He expresses disdain for the Gnostics—those who sought knowledge in religion through reason or empiricism rather than through faith. Although he is influenced by such theologians as Tillich, Niebuhr, Kierkegaard, and Buber, who did engage in philosophical debates, it is their emphasis on a personal relationship to God, on the ideals of love and justice, not on theological speculation, that makes them congenial to him. His is, as he frequently says, a simple faith of simple truths based on love with simple justice that any person can understand.

Reporters have tested the literalness of his scriptural belief. On a few occasions, to this reporter's knowledge, he interpreted the Bible broadly.

During an interview on March 28, 1976, John Hart of NBC News asked: "On the new status of woman . . . I came across Paul's letter to the Ephesians in which he said, 'Wives, submit yourselves unto your own husbands, as unto the Lord. For the husband is the head of the wife, even as Christ is head of the church' [5:22–23]. Does that cause you problems?"

"I don't agree with that concept of the husbands being dominant over the wives," Carter said. "Although I hate to admit there's part of the Bible with which I disagree, that's a passage I've never been able to accept even though

I've tried. My wife doesn't accept it either." Actually, Carter had overlooked the preceding verse (5:21) that all Christians, men and women alike, are to be servants of one another—a radical concept indeed.

In the break between Sunday school and the worship service at the Plains Baptist Church on October 24, 1976, reporters talked to Carter about the lesson. The conversation turned to the Bible. The reporters asked whether he believed the earth is flat, whether he believed in the Garden of Eden and the serpent, whether Eve was taken out of Adam's rib. Carter replied that he did not believe that the earth was square or that it was created in seven 24-hour days.

"Part of the Bible obviously was written in allegories," he said, adding that the Bible was not sexist and reminding his listeners that Jesus "was committed on an equal basis to women."

Two days later, a letter to the editor appeared in the *Atlanta Constitution*.

"The article in Monday's *Atlanta Constitution* incorrectly states that I do not 'believe in such biblical accounts as Eve being created from Adam's rib and other such miracles.' I've never made such a statement and have no reason to disbelieve Genesis 2:21–22 or other biblical miracles. Other newspapers quoted accurately the reporter's question, 'Have you ever had to explain to your children how God created women from Adam's rib?' to which I replied: 'No, I haven't.' " The letter was signed "Jimmy Carter."

Carter may feel himself to be the intellectual equal—perhaps superior—of any politician or leader in the world. But for truly relaxing moments, he finds himself most comfortable with his own family or his church family.

Among the few times he has gone out socially in Washington, he went to the home of his pastor, Dr. Charles Trentham, for dinner, and stayed an hour later than he had planned, unusual for a man who always schedules his time precisely and punctually. One of the dramatic contrasts during the 1976 campaign was to observe Carter speaking with careful correctness to a group of oil executives in Texas and the next day seeing him work easily among his farmhands, both black and white, in the muddy job of draining the pond at his mother's country home. It was easy to see where he felt most at ease. "I feel just as much at home around Billy's filling station as I do in a black church, as I do with big-shot Texas businessmen," he remarked to reporters June 14, 1976, on the campaign plane.

Carter made family life, so important in the life of the Christian church, the subject of his first campaign speech. He said in Manchester, N.H., on August 3, 1976, "The family was the first church. The family was the first school. The family was the first government. If we want less government we must have stronger families, for government steps in by necessity when families have failed." He said every federal program should be analyzed in terms of its impact on the family. And when he spoke to employees at the Department of Housing and Urban Development as president, he said, "Those of you who are living in sin, I hope you will get married." After the laughter died down, he added, "I think it's very important that we have stable family lives. I am serious about that." Carter remarked at a news conference that although he personally practiced monogamy, if some of his staff or cabinet "have slipped from grace, then I can only say that I'll do the best I can to forgive them and pray for them" (news confer-

[18]

ence, June 30, 1977). Fidelity is essential to marriage—"a lifetime commitment," in Carter's words. He told the couples' class at the Washington church on June 12, 1977, that married couples should make "a lifetime commitment" to one another and be faithful through separations, disappointments, even infidelities by one or the other spouse. During times when fidelity is abused, "when a husband or wife succumbs to temptation, that's when faithfulness is paramount."

Fidelity to the church family is important to him, as well. He told the men's class at the Plains Baptist Church on September 5, 1976, on the eve of his formal campaign for the presidency: "This is my church; if there's one thing that gives stability and continuity to my life in the hurly-burly and pressure of a political campaign, it's coming home to Plains every weekend, coming to my church and listening to my teacher."

On a typical Sunday morning in Plains, he and his wife would leave home a few minutes before 10 A.M. to drive to the white clapboard, steepled Plains Baptist Church. There he and his wife would separate to go to the all-men and all-women classes. Carter joined twelve or fifteen longtime friends and neighbors—among them, Clarence Dodson, business manager at South Georgia Tech and class teacher for thirty years; Frank Williams, his business competitor; and P. J. Wise, the father of one of his top aides. Wise, generally, asks the class opening questions—how many had read their Bibles daily during the week? How many had studied the lessons? Jimmy Carter raised his hand each time. He often was asked to give the opening prayer.

About once a month on Saturday night Carter telephoned Dodson to say he would teach the class the next day. The lesson came from the Sunday-school adult lesson book prepared by the Sunday School Board of the Southern Baptist Convention. I have heard the President teach eight or ten times—first in Plains and now at the First Baptist Church in Washington. He speaks informally and makes frequent personal reference. He asks rhetorical questions, not hesitating to ask others to agree or disagree with the answers. His lessons are saturated with Scripture.

After the class in Plains, Carter and his wife would join each other for the morning service, sitting in the third pew from the front on the right-hand side. Frequently he was asked to offer the layman's prayer or benediction. He prays typically for forgiveness of sins, for the constant presence of the Holy Spirit, for Christian unity. In Washington, Carter and his wife go together to Sunday school; there they sit in the second pew in the balcony, where the now-overflowing Sunday-school class is held, and afterward in the sixth pew on the right-hand side of the church for worship.

Carter's presence has created problems for the church he loves. "We have a little bit of a problem worshiping as a First Family," he told the men's class at the First Baptist Church in Calhoun, Georgia, on Easter Sunday, 1977. "Large crowds follow me around. It's almost done severe damage to our little church in Plains. I hope you'll pray for them. They've had a lot of problems. . . . It gives me a sense of humility that my own shortcomings are significant because I'm president. . .

"I enjoyed being a student this morning. I know that sometimes when we come to visit a church, it disrupts the service and causes unnecessary furor. It brings a lot of people to church and Sunday school who don't normally

[come]. I'm just like you are. The fact that I was elected president doesn't make me any better than you are or closer to God. It makes me the target or beneficiary of a lot of prayer."

Carter said he gets letters every day from people who say they are praying for him. "I hope you do the same. When I say something, do something, it has a great effect on people's lives both international and relating to the next-door neighbor. I want to do a good job as president. The responsibilities of the office are great and there are hundreds of things I have to think and decide upon every week that I didn't have to do as a farmer down in Plains. I am close to God. I do pray often and seek his guidance before I make a major decision. My strong Christian beliefs and the fact I do pray to God for guidance does stand me in good stead. It means a lot that the Christian community not only here in this country but around the world give me support through prayer. . . . I pray every day I don't disappoint you and do anything that will make you ashamed."

Carter is a firm believer in foreign missions. He said to worshipers at the First Baptist Church of Lagos, Nigeria, early in April 1978, that "to the extent that missionary effort followed the teachings of Christ, it has been good and benevolent and filled with love." His Washington Sunday-school teacher, Fred Gregg, told UPI's Laurence McQuillan that after leaving the White House Carter plans to spend a year or two as a missionary. Gregg quoted Carter as saying: "I don't want to wake up ten or fifteen years from today and find a country that is friendly to us that has turned to the other side just because some missionary did not do the job he could have done. I would like to be part of being able to turn that country back to God and back to our side and I hope that someday that's what I'll get to do." Asked about it at a news conference, Carter flashed a smile and said he hadn't decided. But he didn't rule it out. He videotaped an appeal to the Southern Baptist Convention in which he urged his fellow parishioners to increase the short-term volunteer mission program. "I have done very little compared to others, but I can and will support a volunteer missionary for two years," he said. "I hope that we will not be timid. Every commitment of our church life should be reexamined and magnified, and we should seek God's guidance and support." He said in a speech to the Southern Baptist Missionary Service Corps in spring 1978, "I wish, in a way, I was free to do more. After my service in my present office . . . I intend to do more." He does not, however, believe in imposing his belief on others. Among his closest staff and his own children, few, if any, have witnessed for Christ with Carter's vigor.

3. Integrating Carter's Faith

There long has been a tension in the Christian faith between personal religion and the outside world. How much of religion consists in loving God, and how much in loving others? Or are these two loves inseparable? How are personal beliefs related to treatment of others? How can love of God and Christ be translated concretely into compassion for real human beings? How are personal beliefs related to government and the structures of society? What does the Bible have to say about the exercise of political power? What guidance can prayer give? Is the love of God or of others incompatible with the exercise of political power? What effect does private morality have on public morality? How is the sanctuary related to the market-place? What does Athens have to say to Jerusalem?

The Apostle Paul told the Philippians (4:11), "I have learned, in whatsoever state I am, *therewith* to be content." Does religion support the economic, social, and political status quo or should a Christian seek to revolutionize society? The Bible seems to set ethical absolutes of love, truth, and justice but also allows a diversity of means to those ends. The prophet Jeremiah quoted Jehovah as saying (1:10), "See, I have this day set thee over the nations and over the kingdoms, to root out, and to pull down, and to destroy, and to throw down, to build, and to plant." But can a person use the "establishment," the existing institutions and governing bodies, with all their flaws and frailties, to accomplish God's will in the world? The person in authority, Paul told the Romans, "is God's servant for your good" (RSV 13:1–7).

Each of these options, according to this writer's sense of scripture, is valid, in the sense of alternative means to a goal which itself is not relative. The Holy Spirit solves the problem by calling some persons to be revolutionaries, some to be entrenched in the establishment, but all to be servants of others and all to be serene in the grace of God.

In the case of Jimmy Carter, what does the Sunday school at the Baptist church have to do with his decisions in the Oval Office? Carter classifies himself with Isaiah and Jeremiah in the Old Testament, "who pronounced God's judgment in the very center of political power." He follows Paul's New Testament teachings that God's will can be carried out in government; that God's will, indeed, should "shape government." More than most other politicians, he has sought to integrate his personal beliefs and public policies. But he has been severely criticized by some Christians and others for being both a creation and an exponent of the establishment. He has been severely criticized for not matching his language about love with vigorous action to help the poor and the needy. How is this criticism reconciled with the fact that he has raised the consciousness of Americans about faith and morality and human rights more than any politician in recent history?

The Bible directs the Christian to love all people everywhere in the world. If our love is to be directed only toward those whom we know or with whom we have personal relationships, we will love only about o.ooooi per cent of the world's people. From Scripture's repeated admonition to care for the widow, the orphan, and the stranger, and Christ's command, "Go ye into all the world and preach the gospel to every creature" (Mark 16:15), we may infer that we are to love everyone. Time and again during his 1976 campaign, Carter spoke of love and compassion and service. In his acceptance speech at the Democratic National Convention in New York and a few days later while teaching Sunday school at the Plains Baptist Church, he drew the vital connection between love and justice.

"Love in isolation doesn't mean anything," he told his classmates (Plains Baptist Church, July 18, 1976). "But love, if applied to other people, can change their lives for the better through simple justice—fairness, equality, concern, compassion, redress of grievances, eliminations of inequalities, recognizing the poor are the ones who suffer most in our society, which is supposed to be fair. There's a great responsibility for those of us who believe in Christ. For us just to sit in isolation and say blandly 'I love everybody' means nothing."

Carter said that loving people, including "those who are poor, uneducated, unemployed, old, sick, black, or who don't speak English," as he expressed it to the black preachers in Atlanta, means assuring them justice. In his view, that's what politics is all about. He frequently quotes Niebuhr's statement, "The sad duty of politics is to establish justice in a sinful world."

Carter views power as servanthood, a radical notion indeed. A few days after he took office, he remarked to employees of the Department of Health, Education and Welfare, "I recognize that I ought to be not 'First Boss' but 'First Servant.'" He had expanded on that concept at the 1977 National Prayer Breakfast where he paraphrased Jesus' words that "whosoever will be chief among you, let him be your servant" (Matthew 20:27). Carter has found personal meaning in Christ's symbolic act of servanthood—the washing of his disciples' feet (John 13); he has spoken of it in his Sunday school classes in Plains and Washington as a demonstration of a leader's relationship to his followers.

The idea of power exercised as servanthood is not easily understood or explained. It seems contradictory. The gathering and exercise of power is the ultimate aphrodisiac, something well understood in Washington. The abuse of power sometimes seems as common as its use for good. Frequently power is used to manipulate people or control events. The vulnerability of people in power to the abuse of power was perhaps the ultimate cause of Watergate. When Jesus was tested by Satan at the start of his ministry, his initial temptation was not sex or wealth but power (Matthew 4:8–10).

Yet the origins of power as servanthood go all the

way back to the Old Testament, where the prophet Isaiah spoke of the coming Messiah as being the suffering servant:

> The Spirit of the Lord GOD is upon me; because the LORD
> hath anointed me to bring good tidings onto the meek;
> He has sent me to bind up the brokenhearted,
> To proclaim liberty to the captives,
> And the opening of the prison to them that are bound;
> To proclaim the acceptable year of the Lord and the day of
>   vengeance of our God;
> To comfort all that mourn.
>
> *(Isaiah* 61:1–2)

When Jesus Christ began his ministry in his hometown of Nazareth, he quoted Isaiah's words (Luke 4:18). Although Jesus was described in regal terms as the King of Kings and the Prince of Peace, his concern always was for the poor in spirit, those who mourn, the meek, those who hunger and are thirsty, the peacemakers (Sermon on the Mount, Matthew 5–7). The Old Testament "holiness code" in Leviticus 19–20 defines holiness in earthbound terms. People were not to steal or lie; they were not to oppress wage earners; they were not to tolerate injustice; they were to love strangers as themselves; they were to help provide for the poor and the sojourner. This is what holiness is all about. Concern for three groups of persons—widows, orphans, and strangers—is expressed repeatedly throughout the Old Testament prophets and in some of the New Testament epistles. It was not a standard that God set merely for the Christian, but rather it was stated as a universal law of justice.

Carter has drawn upon this body of truths frequently.

To a chorus of "Amen's" in his address to the black preachers in Atlanta, he said:

"There is a close correlation between worship services and correcting wrongs. That's what the Bible teaches, because Jesus Christ never hid himself seven days a week in the synagogue. He walked the streets. He touched blind eyes. He healed those who were crippled. He pointed out injustice. He brought about compassion and brotherhood and love. And he changed lives. . . ."

Carter's thoughts on living out love as justice through the ministry of compassion were put to the test in one of the places he loved above all others—his church in Plains. Plains is in the west end of Sumter County, a part of the "Black belt," that arc of rural southern counties stretching across Georgia, Alabama, and Mississippi in which the population has been more than 50 per cent black. In the east end of the county is Andersonville, the Civil War prison site where more than twelve thousand Union soldiers are buried. He had been raised in the predominantly black hamlet of Archery, along the railroad tracks just southwest of Plains. His and one other family were the only whites in a community of twenty-five families. He played with black children. "We used to wrestle, fight, fish, and swim and have footraces and play ball," he told reporters on June 14, 1976, on the campaign jet, though his sister Ruth recalls the black children were conditioned to let the white children win at all the games, which gave the white children a false feeling of superiority and security. The Plains Baptist Church was founded in 1848 as an integrated congregation and blacks left in 1871 during Reconstruction. Through the turbulent years of the 1950s and 1960s, it remained all-white.

The summer of 1962 was long and hot in South Georgia. Martin Luther King, Jr., was jailed in Albany, forty miles from Plains. There was a Ku Klux Klan rally. Freedom riders were fired upon. In late August and early September, four black churches were burned down only a few miles south of Plains. On October 1, Jimmy Carter announced for the state senate, his first elective office. According to newspaper accounts and conversations with persons in the area at the time, Carter said nothing one way or the other about the racial incidents. In 1965, however, Carter, his family, and one other person, who was hard of hearing and did not understand the vote, were the only members of the congregation to stand in voting to permit free entry of any blacks who wanted to attend worship services peacefully. There the matter stood until the month before the 1976 election.

Between Sunday school and the morning worship services of October 24, 1976, Carter paused to chat with reporters. Helen Thomas of UPI, who puts the tough question without fear, asked whether blacks were welcome. Carter pointed out that the church had been integrated until 1875, and that he believed blacks, "if they wanted to," could join the congregation now.

Clennon King, a part-time minister and black activist from Albany, challenged Carter's statement the next Sunday. The deacons called off the service on the Sunday before the election. Carter's news conference in Sacramento, California, his last before the voting began, was consumed by the controversy.

"I think my best approach is to stay within the church and to try to change the attitudes which I abhor. Now if it was a country club I would have quit," he said. "But this is not my church, it's God's church. And I can't quit my lifetime of worship habit and commitment because of a remnant of discrimination which has been alleviated a great deal in the last ten years."

After the election, with Carter present and saying his church was more important to him than the presidency, the congregation voted to allow blacks to join the church. But the controversy was not over. After the inauguration and with Carter in Washington, the congregation voted to fire pastor Bruce Edward, a strong supporter of Carter and desegregation. A group led by Carter's cousin, Hugh, Sr., who was the song leader and the congregation clerk, left to establish a new congregation, the Maranatha Baptist Church, south of Plains.

"It's my church, and I don't ever intend to leave it," he said. But although he said he would return to Plains about once a month as President, he spent only two Sundays in his hometown during the first year after that. On his first visit there after the split, in August 1977, he went to Sunday school at the Plains Baptist Church and to worship services at the Maranatha Baptist Church.

Carter has made human rights the centerpiece of foreign policy. Here, too, he found its origins in scripture.

"In large measure, the beginnings of the modern concept of human rights go back to the laws and the prophets of the Judeo-Christian traditions," he told the World Jewish Congress on November 2, 1977. "I've been steeped in the Bible since early childhood, and I believe that anyone who reads the ancient words of the Old Testament will find . . . the idea of equality before the law and the supremacy of law over the whims of any ruler; the idea of the dignity of the individual human being and also the individual conscience; the ideas of service to the poor and to the oppressed; the ideas of self-government and tolerance and of nations living together in peace, despite differences of belief."

He has confronted directly in a few speeches the traditional conflict in American society between freedom and equality. It is a conflict that he believes must and can be reconciled. He told Asian officials on October 5, 1977, during his United Nations visit, that he "noticed expansion of the definition of human rights in my own consciousness to encompass the right of someone to have a place to work and a place to live and an education and an absence of disease, and, perhaps, an alleviation of hunger." He repeated that thought frequently during his trip to South America and Africa in the spring of 1978.

Some critics have questioned, however, just how much of an impact the demands of Carter's faith have had on his performance in office.

When Carter talked to black audiences during the campaign, he spoke in almost pastoral tones of concern. Much of campaigning was "cold, impersonal" he said of the election. But with black audiences there was feeling. "Some reporters could never figure it out," he said. "It was the common faith we shared" that joined him and blacks together. Nevertheless, black unemployment a year after he entered the White House remained almost twice that of whites. He had made jobs the No. 1 domestic issue, but his support of a full employment bill was only halfhearted. Was not this, in effect, violating the prophetic injunction "not to oppress the wage-earner" (Malachai 3:5 RSV)? His phrase in a press conference that "life is unfair" was, to many blacks, a personal blow. Carter had said he would stop the United States from being arms merchant to the world. Yet, arms sales to other nations continued in the billions of dollars, and despite his campaign statements to the contrary, he spent an increasing amount of money to arm the United States. How could this be reconciled with Jesus' words about peacemakers (Matthew 5:9)? His talk about human rights shifted from addressing specific situations in countries abroad to more general comments.

Was he failing to carry out the truly radical nature of the Christian faith that seeks to renew not only individuals but institutions and nations as well or was he, in effect, reducing the gospel to mere personal qualities with no relevance to the behavior of a nation pursuing wealth and the weapons of war? In one sense, these critics perform the legitimate prophetic role of continually testing the president. They have a right to hold him to the demands of the gospel he himself has articulated. The actions of a president no less than any other person speak louder than his words.

But, in another sense, the modern religious prophets who fault Carter for failing to practice what he preaches enjoy a luxury he does not. They can criticize him with the knowledge that their own words do not really affect others as directly. Every Carter word, every Carter action is carefully analyzed not only in this country but by the nations of the world. What he does affects many others. He must deal with the intricate and fragile nature of diplomacy. He must reconcile and balance the conflicting forces of unemployment, inflation and the budget, of consumers and conservationists, of conglomerates and factory workers, of farmers, middlemen, and grocery shoppers. Prayer does not offer formulas for public policy.

Dag Hammarskjöld's *Markings*, published in 1964, three years after the U.N. Secretary-General's death in Africa, is a powerful book of one man's spiritual journey. Yet it offers few if any clues to the tumultuous events in which he had been involved. One finds no references in *Markings* to U.S. prisoners of war in China, to the Suez or the Congo, in which Hammarskjöld toiled so mightily for peace. Perhaps there is a parallel in Carter's life. During the interview with the National Religious Broadcasters, Carter was asked what he wanted to be remembered for after his life is over. "I've never asked God to let me win an election or to let me have success in politics," he replied. "I've just said, 'Lord, let my actions be meaningful to you and let my life that you've given me not be wasted. Let it be of benefit to Your Kingdom and to my fellow human beings.' If I had that prayer answered, I think I would be very gratified."

When Carter taught Sunday school the week he introduced his comprehensive energy proposal, which he described as one of the most important of his presidency, he said nothing about energy; he talked instead about salvation, Christ, and prayer. The next day, Jordan's King Hussein, a Moslem, came to the White House for a visit. King Hussein's remarks about Carter, as he stood on the south lawn in the bright sunlight, may have summed up best the bond between Jimmy Carter's personal faith and public policies:

"Few world statesmen in recent memory have so clearly and unmistakably defined the personal responsibility of people in high government positions. You have recognized that those who make decisions on behalf of the nation must reflect a code of behavior equal to that of the nation as a whole."

I. The Life of Faith

On Doubt and Faith

ACCEPTING AND GOING ON

Do you ever have any doubts? About yourself, about God, about life?

I can't think of any. Obviously I don't know all the answers to the philosophical questions and theoretical questions . . . the questions that are contrived. But the things that I haven't been able to answer in a theory of supposition, I just accept them and go on, the things that I can't influence or change. I do have, obviously, many doubts about the best way to answer a question or how to alleviate a concern or how to meet a need. Or how to create in my own life a more meaningful purpose and to let my life be expanded in my heart and mind. So, doubt about the best avenue to take among many options is a kind of doubt. That is a constant presence with me. But doubts about my faith? No. Doubt about my purpose in life? I don't have any doubts about that.

> Interview by Bill Moyers, Public Broadcasting Service, May 6, 1976

AN UNCERTAIN SOUND

THE BIBLE SAYS: "If the trumpet give an uncertain sound, who shall prepare himself to the battle?" As a planner and a businessman, and a chief executive, I know from experience that uncertainty is a devastating affliction in private life and in government.

> Address announcing his candidacy for president, National Press Club, Washington, D.C., December 12, 1974. Carter was quoting I Corinthians 14:8.

CONFIDENCE IN SELF

Mr. President, do you ever sit down and reflect on the day's events and what's going on in the world and think, "My God, this is a bigger job than I expected it to be, I'm not sure that I'm up to this"? Do you ever have those moments of self-doubt?

I have sober thoughts when I'm not sure that I can deal with problems satisfactorily. But I have a lot of confidence in myself. Sometimes I go in a back room and pray a while. And a few times I've walked through this mansion where every president has lived, except George Washing-

ton, since 1801 and I've thought about the difficulties and
the tragedy that existed in the lives of many of them and
feel myself to be fortunate. I don't feel inadequate because
I feel that even political opponents want me to succeed.

> Question by Tom Brokaw, NBC News, in an interview
> with President Carter by reporters for the four television
> networks, the White House, December 28, 1977

TILLICH, ON DISTANCE FROM GOD

WE MUST CONSTANTLY SEARCH for ways to make our own
lives more significant and more meaningful, regardless of
our apparent lack of talent or influence. A great modern-
day theologian, Paul Tillich, said in one of his profound
books that religion is the search for the truth about man's
existence and his relationship to God, . . . that when we
think we know it all and are satisfied with what we have
accomplished in the eyes of God, we are already far from
God.

> *Why Not the Best?* (Nashville, Tenn.: Broadman Press,
> 1975), p. 135.

NOT MYSTERIOUS OR MYSTICAL OR MAGICAL

Playboy: *Both the press and the public seem to have made an
issue out of your Baptist beliefs. Why do you think this has happened?*

Carter: I'm not unique. There are a lot of people in this country who have the same religious faith. It's not a mysterious or mystical or magical thing. But for those who don't know the feeling of someone who believes in Christ, who is aware of the presence of God, there is, I presume, a quizzical attitude toward it. . . .

> Interview by Robert Scheer, *Playboy*, November 1976.
> Copyright © 1976 by *Playboy*.

SACRIFICE, DISCIPLINE, PATIENCE

A CHRISTIAN MUST HAVE the willingness of a soldier to give his life . . . the discipline of an athlete to train . . . and the patience of a farmer who plows in hope.

> Couples' Class, First Baptist Church, Washington, D.C., June 12, 1977

WE CAN MOVE MOUNTAINS

WE ARE A COMMUNITY, a beloved community, all of us. Our individual fates are linked, our futures intertwined. And if we act in that knowledge and in that spirit, together, as the Bible says, we can move mountains.

> State of the Union address, the Capitol, January 19, 1978.
> Carter referred to Matthew 17:20: "If ye have faith as a grain of mustard seed, ye shall say unto this mountain, Remove hence to yonder place; and it shall remove . . ."

On Prayer and Worship

MY MAJOR PRAYER

What drives you?

I don't know exactly how to express it . . . it's not an unpleasant sense of being driven. I feel I have one life to live. I feel God wants me to do the best I can with it. And that's quite often my major prayer: Let me live my life so that it will be meaningful.

> Interview by Bill Moyers, Public Broadcasting Service, May 6, 1976

ALMOST LIKE BREATHING

How do you keep yourself fit in the frenzy of a campaign? Mentally fit? Spiritually fit?

I can't say there is an overt self-initiated effort that is successful. It's a part of my nature, a part of my character; it's a part of my religious faith; it's a sense of equanimity; it's a sense of peace. . . .

At night the last thing I do, every night, is to have a brief period of worship. I've never failed since I began [the campaign] in January to read a full chapter in the Bible every night in Spanish. This has been a good habit to maintain.

And, almost like breathing, during the day I have moments of maybe silent prayer and meditation, not often in a structured way, but asking God for wisdom or sound judgment or compatibility with people who depend upon me or whatever would be appropriate under the circumstances.

Interview by the author, at the Carter home, Plains, Georgia, July 9, 1976

Many presidents have testified that Bible reading and prayer have been essential to them in times of crises. Do you find this to be true in your experience?

Yes, I pray many times during the day: when I'm approaching a new encounter with people or when someone asks me for a special thought or consideration, or when I hear about someone who is afflicted or who is troubled, or when I've made a mistake and I want to avoid that mistake again, or when I'm faced with a responsibility that might affect others' lives. I pray as a routine thing. . . .

Interview by National Religious Broadcasters, Indianapolis, Indiana, October 14, 1976

Playboy: *We've heard that you pray 25 times a day. Is that true?*

Carter: I've never counted. I've forgotten who asked me that, but I'd say that on an eventful day, it's something like that.

Playboy: *When you say an eventful day, do you mean you pray as a kind of pause, to control your blood pressure and relax?*

Carter: Well, yes. If something happens to me that is a little disconcerting, if I feel a trepidation, if a thought comes into my head of animosity or hatred toward someone, then I just kind of say a brief silent prayer. I don't ask for myself but just to let me understand what another's feelings might be. Going through a crowd, quite often people bring me a problem, and I pray that their needs might be met. A lot of times, I'll be in the back seat of a car and not know what kind of audience I'm going to face. I don't mean I'm terror-stricken, just that I don't know what to expect next. I'll pray then, but it's not something that's conscious or formal. It's just a part of my life.

Interview by Robert Scheer, *Playboy*, November 1976.
Copyright © 1976 by *Playboy*.

A QUIET REALIZATION

THE BIBLE SAYS, "Pray without ceasing" [I Thessalonians 5:17]. I don't quite do that. It used to be I would pray maybe once or twice a day, or when I got in trouble! Now it's a much more routine and continuing thing for me. In moments of tension or quietness I have a habit of turning to God in a brief prayer, not just in a time of crisis or difficulty, but in a much more natural way. It means a lot to me. I spent more time on my knees in the four years I was governor than in the entire forty years before that because I felt a responsibility on my shoulders not only for my own family's lives but for five million other people. The decisions I made had much more significance. Prayer is a very important part of my life.

I never have relied on flashes of inspiration or visions or things of that kind to change my life—it's just a quiet realization that if I recognize my own fallibility and my own weaknesses and my own potential for mistakes and my own sinfulness and not try to judge other people but try to make decisions with the interest of other people at heart, that this is a very good thing for a political leader to maintain.

Interview by Pat Robertson, "700 Club," Christian
Broadcasting Network, taped during the 1976 campaign
but telecast after the election and before the inauguration

PETITIONARY PRAYER AND GOD'S WILL

I'VE NEVER ASKED GOD to let me be president.

Just to win the nomination?

I never—I never asked God to let me win a single nomination. Never.

What do you pray then?

I ask God to let me do what's right. And to let me do what's best—that my life be meaningful—in an optimum way, and if I win or lose, I believe I can accept the decision with composure, and without regrets, without animosities or hatreds or deep disappointment even.

Interview by Bill Moyers, Public Broadcasting Service, May 6, 1976

I presume you prayed a great deal about your decision to enter the presidential race?

Yes. I never have in my life said a prayer, "Let me succeed." I never said a prayer, "Let me be elected president." I don't think I'm anointed to be president. But I do ask God to let me do the right thing, whether I win or lose.

Do you feel God led you to enter the race? Did you feel the Lord leading strongly?

I can't say that's the case. But I feel at this point, as a candidate, that I'm doing the right thing whether I'm elected or not. I don't feel any constraint that I should be doing something else that's more important or something else that's more decent. There's no conflict at all in my performance as a Christian and my performance in public affairs, and I'm sure there would not be any conflict if I espoused some other belief. I don't feel that God called me to be a candidate or that there's some miraculous prospect that I'm going to be elected because of God's intervention. But I don't feel—

You don't feel you're going against His will to be running?

I do not. I feel I'm doing the right thing by running, whether I win or lose.

> Interview with John Hart, NBC News, March 28, 1976

PRAYER OF CONFESSION

SUPPOSE WE KNEEL DOWN at our bed at night and say, "Lord, forgive me of all my sins. . . ." I don't believe it works unless we're willing to say, "God, today I was not kind to my husband or wife, my children. God, today in a business transaction I cheated a little bit. God, today most of the time I was separated from you. God, today I told two or three lies or misled people a bit. God, today I had a chance to do some kind things or I had a chance to forgive someone I had hatred for and who hurt me. I didn't." Enumerate them! Call them by name. Under those circumstances, all your sins are wiped away.

> Couples' class, First Baptist Church, Washington, April 24, 1977*

PRAYING FOR GUIDANCE

I AM CLOSE to God and I do pray often and seek his guidance before I make any major decision. And my strong

*For text of lesson, see pages 178–187.

Christian beliefs and the fact that I do pray for guidance
stand me in good stead. It means a lot that the Christian
community, not only here in this country but around the
world, gives me support through prayer. . . . I pray
every day that I don't disappoint you or do anything that
will make you ashamed.

> Men's Bible Class, First Baptist Church, Calhoun, Georgia,
> Easter Sunday, April 10, 1977. Carter went to Calhoun to
> spend the Holy weekend. The family had a private sunrise
> service Easter morning.

ON NEEDING PRAYER

YOU'D BE AMAZED at how many times we stand in a receiv-
ing line at the White House or go down a crowd of people
at an airport or when I walked across the front of this
room tonight, and people say, "We pray for you" or
"Every month, our church has a special prayer service for
you." And I say, "Look, make it every week—or every
day—because I really need it."

> To Georgia campaign volunteers, Atlanta, January 20, 1978

PRAYERS FOR AN OPEN HEART,
AN OPEN MIND

OH, LORD, bind our hearts together in Christian love as
we strive for a closer relationship with Christ. [That we

may] have constant love for Thee and all men. . . .
Thank you for the saving grace that comes to us without
regard to how much we deserve it.

We are thankful for Jesus Christ, who paid for our sins.
. . . Thank you for the constant presence of the Holy
Spirit. May it guide us in our daily existence and give us
an open heart, an open mind, unlimited love.

Accept us in Thy Kingdom as humble servants of
Thine, recognizing that what comes to us is from Thee
and through Thee. May we learn about the life of Christ,
that we may come to see it as a perfect example of what
we may attempt to emulate in our daily lives.

Thank you, Father, for the chance to get together and
worship Thee with those we recognize as our brothers and
sisters in Christ. Let there be no disharmony, recognizing
[that] all of us are sinful and forgiven. . . .

Thank you for enjoying one another. Bless this community. Let Christian love be part of our existence. Forgive
us our sins. . . .

> At morning worship, Plains Baptist Church, June 13, 1976,
> the Sunday following victory in the final round of
> presidential primaries

OH FATHER, we stand this morning in Thy presence, we
feel that the Holy Spirit is with us. We know that we are
sinful as are all other people. We know that we deserve
death but also that You love us, that You sent Your Holy
and only Son on earth to be like us and to take the punishment for our sins.

If we believe this, God, with all our hearts and souls,

we know that we can have eternal life and, therefore, have our minds open up to the simple truths, that we can demonstrate our salvation by the attitude that we exhibit toward You and toward our fellow human beings, patterning our lives after Christ. You've given us Your Holy word, the Bible, where we can study in solitude to see what kind of life Christ lived, the perfect example for us all. We thank You for all these things, for the opportunities and the blessings, the challenges and the blessings, that can make our lives worthy in Thy sight, which is the only measurement of the need for our existence. It's a simple thing, Lord, we're thankful for it. Forgive our many sins, through Christ, Amen.

> Men's Bible Class, Plains Baptist Church, July 18, 1976. Carter had accepted the Democratic nomination as president three days before.

PRAYER FOR THE ETERNAL YES

OUR FATHER, we come to the conclusion of another opportunity to learn about Thee. Let our minds be kept open to the message that's been given to us. Let us realize that Christ stands ready, knocking on our hearts to become a part of our eternal life, and although we might have very difficult decisions that we might struggle with or we might have burdens that seem sometimes too hard to bear, although we might have sins that have been a constant oppression on our consciousness for years, all this can be wiped away in just a moment if we accept Christ as our Saviour and open our hearts to Him. He is the eternal yes to our lives. This is the message we've had presented to us. Let our hearts be constantly searching for a close relationship with Thee. . . .

> Benediction, morning service, Plains Baptist Church,
> July 18, 1976

PRAYERS FOR DAILY DISCIPLINE

LET US COME . . . to worship You, opening our hearts to reexamine our sins and shortcomings. May we reestablish a closer relationship with Christ, and be more aware of the needs of our neighbors and our human needs. We have a personal responsibility to represent You. May we have a personal relationship through prayer and study of the word.

> Men's Bible Class, Plains Baptist Church, August 8, 1976

WE OPEN OUR HEARTS to welcome You, to learn more about Thee in orderly and well-planned sermons, in daily, hourly, almost minute-by-minute demonstrations of what Christianity means to us and what the message of Christ can mean in our actions. As we preach our own daily sermons we struggle with the realization of our sinfulness and weakness, seeking to have a fulfilled life. Let us be strong and bold as we try to serve Thee better, in mutual understanding and friendship, recognizing Thy power and glory and worth that can come to all of us.

> Invocation, Sunday morning worship, Plains Baptist
> Church, August 8, 1976

On Prayer and Worship

PRAYER OF REDEDICATION

OUR FATHER, we come together with hearts that need to be opened to receive Thy eternal love and appreciation of our fellow human beings. Let us forget about all other concerns and worries and fears and selfishness and open our hearts and minds to Thy message, recognizing that Your church is the place for us to resubmit our lives to Thee, our sinfulness, weaknesses, shortcomings, to acknowledge them and receive forgiveness through Christ. Let us rededicate our lives, not only every week but every time we acknowledge Thy presence and the presence of the Holy Spirit. We acknowledge our need. . . . We are grateful for Your blessings . . . and we seek the constant knowledge of Your grace through Christ.

> Men's Bible Class, Plains Baptist Church, September 5, 1976. The next day at Warm Springs, Georgia, Franklin Roosevelt's spa, he was to open his campaign for the presidency.

PRAYERS FOR HEALING

It was one of the most difficult days in the long history of the Plains Baptist Church. On the previous Sunday, a cold and damp day, the congregation had voted to desegregate by opening to membership "all persons who want to worship Jesus Christ." Now it was time for reconciliation. Carter was called upon to pray.

[49]

Our Father, we come together with humble hearts and thankful hearts, realizing how You have blessed us, recognizing our sinfulness, weakness, shortcomings, failures, as measured by the perfect life of Christ.

Help strengthen our commitment to observe the Bible teachings so we may help the humble, poor, despised . . . .

Bind our church in close fellowship, help us overcome our difficulties in this church brought about by recent events. Let this be a place of pure and inspired teachings of God's word. May those who come here come with hearts yearning for truth and love; let other motives for coming to our church be wiped out.

> Men's Bible Class, Plains Baptist Church, November 21, 1976

LET EACH [OF US] open our hearts to encompass those around us. You have given us two commandments to love Thee and to love our fellow human beings. We have difficulty often. We've experienced temptation. With Thee nothing is impossible. Forgive our sins, give us wisdom, unselfishness.

Bind our church in a close sense. . . . Let the wounds that have come upon us be healed rapidly. There is no one among us who is better than another. We are all sinful in Your sight. Let us respond in Christ-like fashion because we are being observed closely by the rest of the world. What we do here can rebound with great benefit, or differently . . . .

> Invocation at worship service, Plains Baptist Church, November 21, 1976

PRAYERS FOR CHRISTIAN LOVE

WHEN SO MANY HEARTS are turned to Thee, let us realize the permanence of Thy teaching and the characteristics that are reflected in Jesus' life: simplicity and humility and compassion and love and truth.

We thank Thee for giving Him to us, and as we study about this Christ, Your only Son, we might decide how far short we fall of His perfect example and with Thy forgiveness and Thy love for us even though we are sinners, that we might be encouraged to admit our sins and repent of them, and turn toward Thee, trying always to pattern our lives after Jesus' life.

Draw us near to Thee, to God, and to Thy Christian love. Let us see we are brothers and sisters to all our fellow human beings. And in the spirit of a close-knit family, let us be drawn to one another in a realization of common purposes, common needs, and common blessings that come from Thee. Forgive us this morning our sins and receive our grateful thanks for sending Your Son to this earth.

> Men's Bible Class, Plains Baptist Church, February 13, 1977. It was Carter's first visit home after his inauguration as president.

LET OUR HEARTS BE FILLED with Thanksgiving to realize again that what You mean to us, and what You could mean to us, and still we don't accept. . . . We know we live in sin, we know You still love us, we know You are eager to forgive us if we only accept Thy Son as Saviour.

Christ died on the cross to cleanse us of our sins and we are risen again with Christ in grace. We are able to be Thine again, with Thee. . . . We are thankful for the ministry that can be ours through Jesus Christ; we have the Holy Spirit in our hearts on a daily basis. . . .

We ask Thee, Father, to open our hearts to other people. Help us to accept the two great commandments to love God and love others. We thank You, Lord, that You have seen fit to let us live in a nation where we can worship as we choose. We hope this openness of heart and this ability to be close with God may be a part of the lives of others around the world who still don't know Thy saving grace.

We recognize the torment and pain of Jesus Christ Himself who gave to us the ability to have eternal life. We depend on Thy holiness and purity to give us ultimate salvation. This is the day You've given us; this is the church You've given us.

> Layman's prayer at worship service, Plains Baptist Church, February 13, 1977

PRAYERS FOR RECONCILIATION AND PEACE

President Carter had not been back in Plains for six months. During that interval his church had split in the bitter aftermath of the November 1976 vote to desegregate. Carter resolved the problem of which church to attend by going to both. At both he was asked to pray.

On Prayer and Worship

First he went to the men's Bible class in the Plains Baptist Church, where the teacher, Clarence Dodson, told Carter, "We've missed your influence." Carter gave the opening prayer. Then he went to the seceded church; there he gave the benediction.

Our Father, we come together in Thy house for worship. Let each one search our hearts, help us remove thoughts of jealousy, lack of compassion and love for our fellow human beings. . . .

Deal with those who look to us for leadership as Christians. Help us realize and personify what Christ our Saviour is and was, and realize that we are to set a pattern as Christ set one for us.

God is love, and this feeling of friendship and spirit of companionship and love is a central part of Christianity. Bless all the members of this church and Christians around the world who share brotherhood and sisterhood in God by Christ.

We ask Thy blessings on this country as we struggle for the right to have a decent way of life. Let our nation have the humility to recognize our shortcomings and failures.

Bind our hearts together and help us serve you every day of our lives.

Men's Bible Class, Plains Baptist Church, August 7, 1977

O FATHER BLESS this small and new church. Separate it, we all pray, not out of a sense of alienation and hatred, but out of love and rededication to Thee. Help all tensions to be alleviated. Let there be a genuine search for reconciliation with the Plains Baptist Church. Let it not be a sign of weakness in Thy kingdom, but a sign of strength. Let there be a permanence based on love and forgiveness and rededication.

Benediction, Marantha Baptist Church, August 7, 1977

OUR FATHER, we know nothing could be more appropriate on this birthday of the Prince of Peace than for us each to seek that feeling in our own lives and all human beings. We pray we might remove from our consciousness any feeling of divisiveness or hatred or misunderstanding, or an absence of an ability to communicate on a level of compassion and understanding.

You sent Your Son to be with us, to set an example for us, and we are deeply thankful for this opportunity to learn about Him. With Christ as part of our lives we have an opportunity to exhibit what belief in You means: Subservience to Thy will, a desire to think of others and not of ourselves, an absence of pride, a realization of our need for humility, a desire to have brotherhood and sisterhood exemplified throughout the world.

So in Your holy name we pray this morning that we might realize peace on earth and good will to all human beings who join to us and with us in worshiping Thy name.

Benediction, Marantha Baptist Church, Christmas Day, 1977. Carter had first attended the Men's Bible Class at the Plains Baptist Church. Israeli Prime Minister Menachem Begin and Egyptian President Anwar Sadat were meeting that day to talk about peace.

PRAYER FOR A COMMON LOVE

OUR FATHER GOD in heaven, as we assemble here this morning, opening our hearts to learn the true meaning of our faith, the humility of Christ, the love of Christ, the concern of Christ for those who are in need, let us strive ever more deeply to live according to the example He has set.

Let us be humble before Thee, recognizing our own conceits, our own selfishness, removing hatred from our hearts, sharing our knowledge of the salvation through Christ with our fellow human beings, and setting an example in our own life others might wish to adopt for themselves.

Forgive us, Father, our many sins. And although the oceans and vast lands might separate us one from another, let our hearts be bound together in a common love for Thee.

Let us live in accordance with Thy teachings.

Let us reexamine our own lives.

Let us rededicate ourselves to Thy service as we serve our fellow human beings.

We ask these things, O Father—the blessings of Thy love, forgiveness for our sins. . . .

Prayer at morning worship, First Baptist Church, Lagos, Nigeria, April 3, 1978

On Inner Peace

DOING GOD'S WILL

How do you know the will of God?

I pray many times a day. When I have a sense of peace and just self-assurance—I don't know where it comes from—that what I'm doing is the right thing, I assume, maybe in an unwarranted way, that that's doing God's will.

> Interview by Bill Moyers, Public Broadcasting Service, May 6, 1976

REASSURANCE IN CRISES

I KNOW THE REASSURANCE I get from my own religion and it helps me to take a more objective viewpoint and a calmer approach to crises. I have a great deal of peace with myself and with other people just because of my religious convictions. I think that sort of personal attitude—environment—within which I live helps me to do a better job in dealing with the transient and quite often controversial decisions that have to be made in political life, or in business life, or in family life.

Interview by Ralph Blodgett, *Liberty*, September–October 1976

AT HOME WITH MYSELF

When members of the press are calling out questions, many trying to trick you in your words, many trying to go along with you, some completely neutral, do you find the presence of God in a situation like that? There has to be inner peace to keep up with that.

Well, I have the inner peace. A lot of the newspeople don't understand that phraseology and I don't try to inject it. . . . Quite often a sense of peace is described as superb self-confidence.

I have my own doubts—like everyone else does—about my own abilities or success. But I'm able to accept, I think, with a great deal of equanimity, the prospect of defeat or failure. . . . I can face either victory or defeat without any tensions or fear. This has been translated in the minds of some newspeople as being self-confident or even as arrogance. To me, at least, it's just a sense of being at home with myself and realizing the presence of God in my life.

Interview by Pat Robertson, "700 Club," Christian Broadcasting Network, during the 1976 campaign

ON CARING

What's the most significant discovery Jimmy Carter has made?

. . . This is embarrassing a little bit for me to talk about it, because it's personal, but in my relationship with Christ and with God, I became able in the process to look at it in practical terms, to accept defeat, to get pleasure out of successes, to be at peace with the world. . . . Quite often I'll shake hands with a woman who works in a plant, say, an older woman, and I'll just touch her hand; quite frequently they'll put their arms around my neck and say, "God bless you, son," or, "good luck. I'll help you. Good luck." It's a kind of a relationship with people around me, but I don't want to insinuate that I'm better than other people. I've still got a long way to go, but you asked me a difficult question. What was the major discovery of my life. That's a hard thing to answer.

But you care, though. You do—

I care.

Interview by Bill Moyers, Public Broadcasting Service, May 6, 1976

ON FEAR OF FAILURE

IT'S DEEPLY FELT and sure. My faith in Christ has grown
with age and responsibility. It's much more personal in
nature now. . . . It's only been in the last ten to fifteen
years I've begun to see much more clearly the teachings of
Christ and of the Bible and how they might be translated
into personal action. I have a much deeper sense of security and peace.

I recognize my own fallibilities and weaknesses much
more clearly. I'm not proud any more as I was—in the
past, at least. I was afflicted by pride. I recognize my own
sinfulness and the fact that I can't be perfect as a human
being but that with God's presence and the presence of the
Holy Spirit I can strive ever more effectively to pattern
my own life after the teachings of the Bible.

I've also been blessed in many ways by God's grace
with a stable family, with success in some of the things
that I've attempted. I don't feel so fearful of failure. It
used to be that when I failed in anything I would get
angry with the world and lash out at other people and try
to blame my inabilities on anyone but myself. When I was
successful I didn't get much gratification out of it and I
took all the credit for myself. I think I've been able to look
at my own life in a much more objective way and to subjugate myself to God more. It's just a very great blessing
that God has given me. . . .

Interview by Pat Robertson, "700 Club," Christian
Broadcasting Network, during the 1976 campaign

INNER PEACE IS NOT GUARANTEED

YOU CAN'T SAY, "Tomorrow, I'm going to have inner peace in my heart. . . ." It slips away from us. It's not something guaranteed to each of us. If we subjugate our lives to God, if we open our hearts to the Holy Spirit, if our life is consistent with the purposes or example of Christ . . . in our relationship with God and others, then we will have inner peace. . . .

Couples' Class, First Baptist Church, Washington, D.C., January 29, 1978*

*For text of lesson, see pages 214–224.

On Death and Eternal Life

THE PURPOSE OF LIFE

What do you think we're on earth for?

I don't know. I could quote the biblical references to creation, that God created us in His own image, hoping that we'd be perfect, and we turned out to be not perfect but very sinful. And then when Christ was asked what are the two great commandments from God which should direct our lives, He said, "To love God with all your heart and soul and mind . . . and love your neighbor as yourself" [paraphrase of Mark 12:30–31]. So I try to take that condensation of the Christian theology and let it be something through which I search for a meaningful existence. I don't worry about it too much any more. I used to when I was a college sophomore, and we used to debate for hours and hours about why we're here, who made us, where shall we go, what's our purpose. But I don't feel frustrated about it.

You know, I'm not afraid to see my life ended. I feel like every day is meaningful. I don't have any fear at all of death. I feel I'm doing the best I can, and if I get elected president, I'll have a chance to magnify my own influence, maybe . . . in a meaningful way. If I don't get elected president, I'll go back to Plains. So I feel a sense of equanimity about it. But what—why we're here on earth, I don't know.

Interview by Bill Moyers, Public Broadcasting Service, May 6, 1976

THE UNIMPORTANCE OF THE LENGTH OF LIFE

I WOKE UP EARLY this morning and read again from the *Bhagavad-Gita* for a couple of hours. It's a beautiful work. . . . on the unimportance of the length of physical life.

At the Rashtrapati Bhavan, New Delhi, India, January 2, 1978, during a conversation with Indian Prime Minister Morarji Desai. Desai had given a copy of the *Bhagavad-Gita*, the sacred writings of the Hindus, to Carter. Carter gave the journals of the American philosopher Henry Thoreau to the prime minister.

CHRIST didn't heal everybody He could [because] He didn't want to emphasize the importance of physical life.

When He healed, He healed not only their physical body [but] forgave their sins.

Response to a question about Jesus (Mark 5:25–34), Couples' Class, First Baptist Church, Washington, D.C., February 6, 1977

PHYSICAL LIFE is not the most important thing in God's eyes. We attach great importance to death, funerals, bereavement, and so forth. If we are Christians, that's the beginning of our promised life with Christ. What Christ was saying was, the destruction of a human being's relations with one another, relations with God, are much more important than even the loss of one's life.

Couples' Class, First Baptist Church, Washington, D.C., August 28, 1977

IF WE THINK that our existence on earth is the most important of all, then to lose it is one of our most important losses. . . . Christ's death and resurrection proved to us that there's life after death, but it also proved to us that preoccupation with the present human life should not be ascendant in our consciousness.

Couples' Class, First Baptist Church, Washington, D.C., January 29, 1978*

*For text of lesson, see pages 214–224.

ASSURANCE OF ETERNAL LIFE

Playboy: . . . *We wonder if you've ever discussed with Rosa-lynn the possibility of being assassinated. And, assuming you have, how do you deal with it in your own mind?*

Carter: Well, in the first place, I'm not afraid of death. In the second place, it's the same commitment I made when I volunteered to go into the submarine force. . . .

Playboy: *Your first answer was that you don't fear death. Why not?*

Carter: It's part of my religious belief. I just look at death as not a threat. It's inevitable, and I have an assur-ance of eternal life. . . .

Interview by Robert Scheer, *Playboy*, November 1976.
Copyright © 1976 by *Playboy*.

ETERNAL LIFE IS NOW

WHAT DIFFERENCE is it if we live fifty-six years or fifty-eight years or seventy-three years or eighty-four years? Sometimes we have such an intense fear of death that we can't really live. The meaning of life is not in the number of years on earth. . . . Martin Luther King, Jr., died a young man. John Kennedy died a young man. The average age of those who wrote the Declaration of Independence was about forty years young. Christ's ministry only lasted for three years. We tend to think that to exist seventy, seventy-five years is a great achievement and very important. But Christ . . . is trying to show that victory over death can give meaning in our life. We should not be preoccupied with physical death; we should not be preoccupied with physical health. We should not be preoccupied with fame and reputation and social status. . . .

When does eternal life begin for us? At death? Are we partaking now of part of our eternal life? Yes. We have too much tendency to say, "Someday, later on, I'm going to be a meaningful person. I'm going to do the things I've always known were right. I'm going to prepare for my life with Christ—someday. But for the time being, I'm going to cling to things given me—security, status, competence, happiness, gratification. ; . ." Let's not wait until the day of our death to start to join the presence of Christ. A lot of people say this, "After death, I'll be with Christ. After death, the Holy Spirit will be part of my existence. After death, I'll know the meaning of God."

Christ says, forget about death and enjoy and appreciate and understand the meaning of life. . . . We don't have to wait until we die, or to come back to life, or a miracle occurs, or we read about a miracle, to know joy, exaltation, fullness of life, celebration, because God has already given it to us. To the extent that our life isn't full, [but is] filled with fear or trepidation or doubt or insecurity, we're wasting it.

[It's] a symbol of selfishness to concern ourselves about the limit of our physical existence. . . . Paul said that all those who believe in Christ have eternal life. Life begins now. Our relationship with Christ is of greater significance to our life than the shortness of our life, the absence of our life. . . . On the day we know Christ our eternal life begins, and the rosy future which we set down when we are going to restructure our lives is now.

Couples' Class, First Baptist Church, Washington, D.C., December 18, 1977*

*For text of lesson, see pages 205–214.

II. Temptation, Sin, Forgiveness, and Grace

On Falling Short

THE DESPAIR AND CHALLENGE OF
FALLING SHORT

THE DESPAIRING ASPECT of it that we as Christians know is that as we measure ourselves against God, we'll fall short. . . . The failure of us all to measure up to God's expectations or man's laws creates a predictable and beneficial anxiety, a concern that we are not measuring up to God's standards. . . . Anxiety is not necessarily a bad word. It creates a tension within ourselves which is an inspiration, a challenge, and a basis for self-condemnation or self-acknowledgment of inadequacy or sin. We try to overcome those anxieties, but, in effect, we never change one for another, we *substitute* one for another . . . and it's because we ought to be anxious about our shortcomings. We ought to be anxious about our lack of love of God. We ought to be concerned about how much more we can know about the world or about people around us.

Couples' Class, First Baptist Church, Washington, D.C., January 29, 1978*

LIKE PETER, UNDER PRESSURE

WHEN WE'RE PUT UNDER PRESSURE in the world around us, even though we know the pure teachings of Christ, even though we know the perfect example of Christ, we do just like Peter did. We yield, we back down, we apologize, we stay silent, under pressure. So we're not in a position to criticize Peter.

Men's Bible Class, Plains Baptist Church, June 20, 1976†

SIN AND JUDGMENT

Playboy: . . . *We still wonder how your religious beliefs would translate into political action. For instance, would you appoint judges who would be harsh or lenient toward victimless crimes—offenses such as drug use, adultery, sodomy and homosexuality?*

Carter: Committing adultery, according to the Bible—which I believe in—is a sin. For us to hate one another,

---

*For text of lesson, see pages 214–224.
† For text of lesson, see pages 156–162.

for us to have sexual intercourse outside marriage, for us to engage in homosexual activities, for us to steal, for us to lie—all these are sins. But Jesus teaches us not to judge other people. We don't assume the role of judge and say to another human being, "You're condemned because you commit sins." All Christians, all of us, acknowledge that we are sinful and the judgment comes from God, not from another human being. . . .

Playboy: *What about those laws on the books that govern personal behavior. . . . Do you think such laws should be on the books at all?*

Carter: That's a judgment for the individual states to make. I think the laws are on the books quite often because of their relationship to the Bible. Early in the nation's development, the Judeo-Christian moral standards were accepted as a basis for civil law. But I don't think it hurts to have this kind of standard maintained as a goal. . . .

Interview by Robert Scheer, *Playboy*, November 1976.
Copyright © 1976 by *Playboy*.

SIN AND HUBERT HUMPHREY

HE AND I talked about religion, about how deep his faith had grown since he became ill. We talked about sin and how we know that "everyone sins and we fall short of the glory of God," but how God forgives us. Just a few days ago I was in India, and I was visiting the memorial to Mahatma Gandhi where his body was cremated. I didn't think about Senator Humphrey—I have to admit it—until

I started to leave. One of the Indian leaders took me over to a wall, and there on the wall was a quote from Gandhi. The title of it was "The Seven Sins." When I saw that, I thought of Senator Humphrey's discussion on sin. According to Gandhi, the seven sins are wealth without works, pleasure without conscience, knowledge without character, commerce without morality, science without humanity, worship without sacrifice, and politics without principle. Hubert Humphrey may have sinned in the eyes of God, as we all do, but according to those definitions of Gandhi's, Hubert Humphrey was without sin.

> Remarks at funeral of Senator Hubert Humphrey, St. Paul, Minnesota, January 16, 1978. Carter was paraphrasing Romans 3:23.

PRIDE AND TEMPTATION

Playboy: *Do you feel you've reassured people with this interview, people who are uneasy about your religious beliefs, who wonder if you're going to make a rigid, unbending president?*

Carter: . . . What Christ taught about most was pride, that one person should never think he was any better than anybody else. One of the most vivid stories Christ told in one of his parables was about two people who went into a church. One was an official of the church, a Pharisee, and he said, "Lord, I thank You that I'm not like all those other people. I keep all Your commandments, I give a tenth of everything I own. I'm here to give thanks for making me more acceptable in Your sight." The other guy was despised by the nation, and he went in, prostrated himself on the floor and said, "Lord, have mercy on me, a sinner. I'm not worthy to lift my eyes to heaven." Christ asked the disciples which of the two had justified his life. The answer was obviously the one who was humble.

The thing that's drummed into us all the time is not to be proud, not to be better than anyone else, not to look down on people but to make ourselves acceptable in God's eyes through our own actions and recognize the simple truth that we're saved by grace. It's just a free gift through faith in Christ. This gives us a mechanism by which we can relate permanently to God. I'm not speaking for other people, but it gives me a sense of peace and equanimity and assurance.

I try not to commit a deliberate sin. I recognize that I'm going to do it anyhow, because I'm human and I'm tempted. And Christ set some almost impossible standards for us. . . .

But I don't think I would *ever* take on the same frame of mind that Nixon or Johnson did—lying, cheating and distorting the truth. Not taking into consideration my hope for my strength of character, I think that my religious beliefs alone would prevent that from happening to me. I have that confidence. I hope it's justified.

Interview by Robert Scheer, *Playboy*, November 1976.
Copyright © 1976 by *Playboy*. The story of the Pharisee is in Luke 18:10–14.

ON DISCARDING PEOPLE

There have been more general charges that when people have worn out their usefulness you dispose of them or that you have been known to hold a grudge.

I am not perfect. Like all human beings I am sinful and I certainly have made mistakes. Most of the people who are now working for me have been with me for a long time. The newcomers to my campaign . . . I think, would testify that there is no inclination on my part to discard people once their usefulness has been terminated. If someone did show me an inability of proper performance in an assigned position or if someone should show me an inability to serve the public well or had some discovered moral defect that I thought would destroy the confidence of the people in a campaign or in the government I would not hesitate to dispose of their services.

> Interview by Jim Castelli, National Catholic News Service, Washington, D.C., August 9, 1976

RUTHLESSNESS

Tom Ottenad, a very well-known writer for the St. Louis Post-Dispatch, *said recently, "In a ruthless business, Jimmy Carter is a ruthless operator. Even as he wears his broad smile and displays his Southern charm." Can you be ruthless in the way I think he means it here? And a Christian?*

I presume—well, I'm a Christian, no matter what.

But how do you reconcile?

Okay, he was talking about the campaign. And I don't know what he meant by ruthless. I don't think I've ever deliberately hurt one of my opponents to gain an advantage. I try not to. I don't remember when I have. There may have been something that I've said in the heat of competition that made them feel discomfited. I can't deny that. But—most people when they get to know me think that—finally decided that I'm much tougher than is originally apparent. So the word "ruthless" to me has connotations of cruelty. And I'm not sure I could be cruel.

Interview by Bill Moyers, Public Broadcasting Service,
May 6, 1976

ON NOT BETRAYING TRUST

I HAVE TO TELL YOU with complete candor that being elected President of the United States is not the most important thing in my life.

There are many other things that I would not do to be president. I would not tell a lie; I would not mislead the American people; I would not avoid taking a stand on a controversial issue which is important to our country or the world. And I would not betray your trust.

Rally at Atlantic Civic Center, December 12, 1974

ON LACK OF COMMITMENT TO GOD

WHEN I WAS A CANDIDATE for public office, particularly the last campaign I ran, I gave a hundred percent of everything in me to win, to let the American people know the good side of my character, perhaps to conceal my defects, to let them realize how badly I wanted to serve.

I didn't waste any time and neither did my family, and neither did many friends. But I have to stand here and confess to you that I have never given that much of a sustained commitment to serving God.

> Southern Baptist Brotherhood Commission, Atlanta, Georgia, June 16, 1978*

JUDGING OTHERS

MORAL STANDARDS, you know, are primarily personal in nature. One of the teachings of Christ in which I believe is that we should not judge other people. One of the tenets of the Christian faith is that all of us are sinners, that we are not—none of us are—better than others, that we are saved by God through grace, which means a free gift, not because of good works that we do. And Jesus Himself taught that we should not judge others. . . . In the Sermon on the Mount [He said] do not be concerned about the mote or the speck that's in your brother's eye when you have beams in your own eye.

> Interview by Harry Reasoner, ABC News, Plains, Georgia, August 2, 1976. The Sermon on the Mount is found in Matthew 5–7. Carter referred specifically to 7:1–2.

IT COMPLETELY VIOLATES all the teachings of Christ to become proud and self-satisfied and to be critical of or judge

*For text of speech, see pages 251–259.

one's fellow human beings. If there is one thought that permeated the teachings of Christ about man's own weakness and sinfulness it was self-pride and self-satisfaction and a feeling of superiority and a feeling of strength in the absence of God's guidance. And if I should be guilty of this accusation . . . then I would be in that respect sinful in the eyes of God.

Interview by Jim Castelli, Catholic News Service, August 9, 1976

TEMPTATION FOR SELF-RECOGNITION

WE DON'T HAVE to pray in public; we don't have to drop our money in the collection plate with a great clatter so everybody sees us; we don't have to push the fact that we love our neighbors. Genuine love can overcome human temptation for self-recognition.

Couples' Class, First Baptist Church, Washington, D.C., January 29, 1978*

THE PLATEAU OF SELF-SATISFACTION

ALL THROUGHOUT LIFE there's got to be searching for a deeper relationship with Christ through the Holy Spirit, a deeper relationship with God through the Holy Spirit, a deeper relationship with our fellow human beings. . . . If

*For text of lesson, see pages 214–224.

we ever reach that plateau: "I have measured up to God's requirements. My life is a success. I'm an adequate Christian," that's when we lose something precious. We need to dig more deeply and grow in the understanding of God.

Couples' Class, First Baptist Church, Washington, D.C., January 29, 1978*

THE SENSE OF LOSS

SOMETIMES WE WITHDRAW from Christ. We go about our daily business grasping for money, pushing people out of the way, telling little white lies, not being quite kind enough to the person we're with. Then, if we're growing Christians, we are conscious of our limitations. We stop a minute and say, "Where am I? What am I doing? I've lost something that stabilizes my life."

Couples' Class, First Baptist Church, Washington, D.C., April 24, 1977†

THE COUNTERFEITS OF LOVE

WE CAN TALK, attend Sunday school, sing hymns, put on a pious attitude, and prove, thereby, that we . . . that we don't really love Christ, we love ourselves. We love the

*For text of lesson, see pages 214–224.
†For text of lesson, see pages 178–187.

approbation that comes to us from Christians as we pretend to love Christ. . . . Love is not a quiescent thing . . . love is an active thing, a demonstrable thing. We can isolate ourselves, not do anything, not hurt anybody—that would not be an expression of love. Love is a difficult thing. It's a precious thing, and, like almost every other precious thing, it has a lot of counterfeits. . . .

Couples' Class, First Baptist Church, Washington, D.C., January 29, 1978*

*For text of lesson, see pages 214–224.

On Repentance and Injury

BE RECONCILED THROUGH LOVE

DR. MARTIN LUTHER KING, SR., said the other night, "If you have any hatred left in your heart, get on your knees, get on your knees. It's a time to wipe away hatred and disharmony and animosities and distrust. Get on your knees and forgive those you feel hate you and vice versa." Jesus said, "If you come to the altar with a gift and you've got hatred in your heart for anybody, set your gift over to the side, go find that person, be reconciled through love, then come back to the altar and worship God" [paraphrase of Matthew 5:23–24]. . . . God can't look on sinfulness and say, "That's okay." God's perfect, God's holy. He can't say, "All you sinful people, what you do is okay with me. Go ahead and sin, I love you anyway. . . ." All who sin—Sunday-school teachers, preachers, priests, bishops, people who never come to church—in God's eyes, we're all sinners. I don't believe God says, "Here's one person who is more sinful than another." I don't think He ranks us in an order. He loves us all. . . . "The wages of sin"—what does God owe us? Death. [Romans 6:23.] But God loves [us] so much that He sent His only Son to take the punishment for our sin. . . . If we have faith in Him, then what can we have? Eternal life. We can be reconciled to God. We can be forgiven for our sins. It's just as though we had never sinned. . . .

If you do that, you'll have eternal life. And in that moment—it's so easy to do—Christ comes into our heart and we have a new life through Christ with God. It's not complicated, there's no trick to it, but it requires humility. . . . In that moment we take Christ in our hearts, we're brothers and sisters with one Father who is God . . . at that moment we begin to demonstrate our love, not with a halo, not in isolation, not in pride, but by showing we love our fellow human beings, the same way Christ loved them, the same way Christ loves us.

Men's Bible Class, Plains Baptist Church, July 18, 1976*

IT WASN'T THE NATURE of his offering that was rejected but what was in Cain's heart. . . . Later on in the New Testament, Jesus said, If you come to the altar with an offering and your brother has aught against you, go first and be reconciled to your brother and then give the offering. It was this absence in Cain himself and his attitude toward God and Abel that were not acceptable—not the offering.

In answer to a question, Couples' Class, First Baptist Church, Washington, D.C., April 23, 1978. The story of Cain and Abel is in Genesis 4; Carter referred to the remarks of Jesus in Matthew 5:24.

*For text of lesson, see pages 162–175.

I WENT DOWN THE LIST in my mind of those who I felt have hurt me and asked God to give them a special blessing.

> To reporters at the Carter family peanut warehouse after a week of campaigning, Plains, Georgia, October 18, 1976

ON SHARING PAIN AND SORROW

ONE OF IRAN'S GREAT POETS, Saadi, wrote: "Human beings are like parts of a body, created from the same essence. When one part is hurt and in pain, others cannot remain in peace and quiet. If the misery of others leaves you indifferent and with no feeling of sorrow, then you cannot be called a human being." . . . This brief passage shows that there is within the consciousness of human beings a close tie with one's neighbors, one's family, and one's friends, but it also ties us with human beings throughout the world. When one is hurt or suffers, all of us, if we are human beings, are hurt and we suffer.

> Quoted by Carter at the state dinner given for the President by the Shah of Iran, Tehran, December 31, 1977. Saadi lived about 600 years ago.

On God's Saving Grace

AS WHITE AS SNOW

GOD STILL LOVES US. If we believe in Him, we can be reconciled to God. If we repent, our lives are washed "as white as snow."

> Men's Bible Class, Plains Baptist Church, December 21, 1976. Carter was quoting Isaiah 1:18.

SAVED BY GRACE

WE'RE NOT SAVED because we're Americans; we're not saved because we come from a community that's stable; we're not saved because our parents were Christians; we're saved because God loves us; we're saved by grace through one required attitude—that's faith in Christ. We're saved by grace through faith in Christ. So is everybody else. So is everybody else.

> Men's Bible Class, Plains Baptist Church,
> June 20, 1976*

NO SECOND-CLASS CITIZENSHIP

I GUARANTEE YOU, Paul guarantees you, Christ guarantees you, God guarantees you, that you will be forgiven. There is no longer any Jew or Gentile, no longer man or woman, no longer man or child, no longer black or white in Christ . . . no longer any second-class citizenship in the Christian church in the eyes of God.

A lot of people want to complicate the issue. . . . We put obstacles in our mind. A person can be saved by accepting God's grace, something we don't deserve, yet we get.

> Men's Bible Class, Plains Baptist Church, July 25, 1976.
> The lesson topic was "The Message of Grace Through
> Faith." Carter cited two of the texts, "The just shall live by
> faith" (Romans 1:17) and "if righteousness *come* by the law,
> then Christ is dead in vain" [Galatians 2:21].

WE NEED NEVER BE FEARFUL OR WEAK

THOUGH WE'RE WEAK, we're resentful, we're doubtful, we're lonely, we're not influential, we're insecure by our-

---

*For text of lesson, see pages 156–162.

selves, we need not ever feel alone. If we are doubtful, filled with anxiety, we need never be fearful, because with Christ, with the Holy Spirit, we're given the strength adequate to meet the responsibilities put on us by God. That's a big responsibility. With the Holy Spirit, with Christ, with God, we are strong enough, forceful enough, competent enough, brave enough to meet the responsibilities of God.

> Couples' Class, First Baptist Church, Washington, D.C., January 29, 1978*

*For text of lesson, see pages 214–224.

III. Religion and Politics

On Love with Justice

SIMPLE JUSTICE

THE TIME FOR RACIAL DISCRIMINATION is over. Our people have already made this major and difficult decision, but we cannot underestimate the challenge of hundreds of minor decisions yet to be made. Our inherent human charity and our religious beliefs will be taxed to the limit. No poor, rural, weak, or black person should ever have to bear the additional burden of being deprived of the opportunity of an education, a job, or simple justice.

Inauguration as governor of Georgia, January 12, 1971

THERE IS A MANDATORY RELATIONSHIP between the powerful and the influential and the socially prominent and wealthy on the one hand, and the weak, the insecure, and the poor on the other hand.

This is a relationship not always completely understood. I don't completely understand it myself. But I know that in a free society we do see very clearly that one cannot accept great blessings bestowed on him by God without feeling an inner urge and drive to share those blessings with others of our neighbors who are not quite so fortunate as we.

Lions' Convention, Jekyll Island, Georgia, June 8, 1971

A GOVERNMENT OF HUMAN BEINGS

NOWHERE IN THE CONSTITUTION of the United States or Declaration of Independence, nor the Bill of Rights, nor the Old Testament, nor the New Testament, do you find the words "economy" or "efficiency." However, you find other words that are much more important—words like self-reliance, words like beauty, and words like appreciation, and words like foresight, and words like stewardship, brotherhood, tenacity, commitment, compassion, and love, that describe what a human being ought to be and also describe what the government of those human beings ought to be.

Address to National Wildlife Federation, Pittsburgh, Pennsylvania, March 15, 1975

JUSTICE IN A SINFUL WORLD

REINHOLD NIEBUHR OBSERVES that the sad duty of politics is to establish justice in a sinful world. He goes on to explain that there is no way to establish or maintain justice without law, that the laws are constantly changing to stabilize the social balance of the competing forces of a dynamic society, and that the sum total of the law is an expression of the structure of government.

> *Why Not the Best?*, 1975, p. 93. Carter spoke similarly in a Law Day address at the University of Georgia, May 4, 1974. Carter was quoting Reinhold Niebuhr, *On Politics* (New York: Scribner's, 1960), p. 180.

LOVE NOT ISOLATED

LOVE IN ISOLATION doesn't mean anything. But love, if applied to other people, can change their lives for the better through what I describe . . . as simple justice—fairness, equality, concern, compassion, redressing of grievances, elimination of inequalities, recognizing the poor are the ones who suffer the most even in our society, which is supposed to be fair. There's a great responsibility for those of us who believe in Christ. For us to sit in isolation and say blandly "I love everybody" means nothing.

> Men's Bible Class, Plains Baptist Church, July 18, 1976. This was the Sunday after Carter won the Democratic party's presidential nomination.*

WE ARE THE RIVERS OF JUSTICE

HAVE WE CREATED CHASMS around ourselves that separate us from those who need and hunger for the gospel of

*For text of lesson, see pages 162–175.

Christ? Is our primary goal in life as Christians to husband to ourselves the mercy of God, the forgiveness of our sins, the knowledge of Christ that gives us truth? Or is it to tear down barriers, to reach out and share, to affect other people's lives in a benevolent way and an unselfish way, and, at the same time, to expand our own lives, instead of being narrow . . . . ?

Sometimes the church creates a barrier itself because we tend to encapsulate ourselves in respectability, security, goodness, decency, religious commitment. Amos said, "I hate and I despise your feasts and your institutions" [paraphrase of 5:21]. He was talking about the church of his day. He said, "Let justice roll down like waters, and righteousness like an ever-flowing stream" [5:24, RSV]. It was hard back in those days for justice and righteousness to roll down like waters out of the church, and it's hard today. Where is the water, where is the ever-flowing stream that can roll down out of the church, filled with righteousness and mercy? Where is that water? Ourselves. We are the rivers of water. We are the ever-flowing stream.

Couples' Class, First Baptist Church, Washington, D.C., November 6, 1977*

JUSTICE THROUGH GOVERNMENT

When your life is over, for what do you want to be remembered?

I would like to have my frequent prayer answered that God let my life be meaningful in the enhancement of His

*For text of lesson, see pages 193–205.

Kingdom and that my life might be meaningful in the enhancement of the lives of my fellow human beings. That I
might help translate the natural love that exists in this
world and do simple justice through government. I believe
that the almost accidental choice of politics as part of my
life's career will have been a very gratifying part of realizing that prayer. I've never asked God to let me win an
election or to let me have success in politics. I've just said,
"Lord, let my actions be meaningful to You and let my life
that You've given me not be wasted. Let it be of benefit to
Your Kingdom and to my fellow human beings." If I had
that prayer answered, I think I would be very gratified.

Interview by National Religious Broadcasters, Indianapolis,
Indiana, October 14, 1976

HUMAN RIGHTS AND THE JUDEO-CHRISTIAN TRADITION

"WHAT DOES THE LORD REQUIRE of you that you do justly
and love mercy and walk humbly with your God." I hope,
as you maintain an attitude of self-introspection and self-
examination, the removal of hatred and prejudice from
your hearts, a recommitment to the finest principles of
love and compassion and brotherhood and simple justice,
in these next few days—that you would think not only
about me and others who might have to serve this country, but about our nation itself. . . . We ought to translate
love for one another into the application of simple justice.
Justice takes on many forms, and although it can be described as simple, it's a complex thing, and the complexity
of it arises from the fact that our nation is made up of so

many people. We're not a melting-pot as has sometimes been described because a melting-pot means that everything blends in together and becomes the same. We're more of a mosaic—a beautiful mosaic—of different kinds of people who have different kinds of background and interests and education and experience and hopes and dreams and aspirations and fears and prejudices. . . .

> To conference of Presidents of Major Jewish Organizations, on Rosh Hashanah, Boston, Massachusetts, September 30, 1976. Carter paraphrased Micah 6:8.

IN LARGE MEASURE, the beginnings of the modern concept of human rights go back to the laws and the prophets of the Judeo-Christian traditions. I've been steeped in the Bible since early childhood, and I believe that anyone who reads the ancient words of the Old Testament with both sensitivity and care will find there the idea of government as something based on a voluntary covenant rather than force—the idea of equality before the law and the supremacy of law over the whims of any ruler; the idea of the dignity of the individual human being and also of the individual conscience; the idea of service to the poor and to the oppressed; the ideas of self-government and tolerance and of nations living together in peace, despite differences of belief. . . .

The Old Testament offers a vision of what that kind of peace might mean in its deepest sense. . . . The lines from the prophet Micah—who's still one of my favorites— are words to which no summary or paraphrase could possibly do justice. . . .

But in the last days it shall come to pass, that the mountain of the house of the Lord shall be established in the top of the mountains, and it shall be exalted above the hills; and people shall flow into it.

And many nations shall come, and say, Come, and let us go up to the mountain of the Lord, and to the house of the God of Jacob; and He will teach us of His ways, and we will walk in His paths: for the law shall go forth of Zion, and the word of the Lord from Jerusalem.

And He shall judge among many people, and rebuke strong nations afar off; and they shall beat their swords into plowshares, and their spears into pruninghooks: nation shall not lift up a sword against nation, neither shall they learn war any more.

But they shall sit every man under his vine and under his fig tree; and none shall make them afraid: for the mouth of the Lord of Hosts hath spoken it.

For all people will walk every one in the name of his god, and we will walk in the name of the Lord our God for ever and ever. [Micah 4:1–5.]

However we may falter, however difficult the path, it is our duty to walk together toward the fulfillment of this majestic prophecy.

> Address to the General Council of the World Jewish
> Congress, Washington, D.C., November 2, 1977

KING, GANDHI, AND NONVIOLENCE

AMONG THE MANY who marched and suffered and bore witness against the evil of racial prejudice, the greatest was Dr. Martin Luther King, Jr. He was a son of Georgia and a spiritual son of Mahatma Gandhi.

The most important influence in the life and work of Dr. King, apart from his own religious faith, was the life of Gandhi. Martin Luther King took Gandhi's concepts of nonviolence and truth-force and put them to work in the American South.

Like Gandhi, King believed that truth and love are the strongest forces in the universe. Like Gandhi, he knew that ordinary people, armed only with courage and faith, could overcome injustice by appealing to the spark of good in the heart even of the evildoer.

Like Gandhi, we all learned that a system of oppression damages those at the top as surely as it does those at the bottom. And for Martin Luther King, like Mahatma Gandhi, nonviolence was not only a political method, it was a way of life and a spiritual path to union with the ultimate.

These men set a standard of courage and idealism that few of us can meet, but from which all of us can draw inspiration and sustenance.

The nonviolent movement for racial justice in the United States, a movement inspired in large measure by the teachings and examples of Gandhi and other Indian leaders, changed and enriched my own life and the lives of many millions of my countrymen.

Address to Indian Parliament, New Delhi, January 2, 1978

EQUALITY OR FREEDOM

I'M A SUNDAY-SCHOOL TEACHER, and I've always known that the structure of law is founded on the Christian ethic that you shall love the Lord your God and your neighbor as yourself—a very high and perfect standard. We all know that the fallibility of man, and the contentions in society, as described by Reinhold Niebuhr and many others, don't permit us to achieve perfection. We do strive for equality, but not with a fervent and daily commitment. In general, the powerful and the influential in our society shape the laws and have a great influence on the legislature or the Congress. This creates a reluctance to change because the powerful and the influential have carved out for themselves or have inherited a privileged position in society, of wealth or social prominence or higher education or opportunity. . . .

Address on Law Day, University of Georgia, May 4, 1974

EVER SINCE OUR COUNTRY WAS FOUNDED we've struggled with the question, how can we have liberty, freedom— and at the same time, equality. These don't naturally go together.

When you have complete freedom, the rich and the powerful overwhelm the poor and the weak. When you have absolute equality guaranteed by the state, quite often you eliminate the concept of individuality and freedom.

Our country has committed itself to providing both. We're moving in that direction slowly, but. . . . In the most important aspect, we're equals. We're brothers and sisters. With hope and confidence we can have liberty, justice, equality.

Mexican Independence Day Rally, Saginaw, Michigan, September 16, 1976

Religion and Politics

WHEN IS WANTING WRONG? The tenth commandment may be at the base of all the other commandments: "Thou shalt not covet what is thy neighbor's." If any commandment is uniquely applicable to the United States and our materialistic society, this is the one.

(Carter asked the class whether freedom or equality was the more important. One member said it was freedom.)

If I was teaching this class in the ghetto of New York, where parishioners can't go to church in an automobile and worry about what their children will have for supper, I think they'd say "equality". . . . There is a natural preference for the powerful and the rich and the good to say "freedom," but for many people in the world who are deprived all they want is to be equal. There has always been a conflict between those two things.

Couples' Class, First Baptist Church, Washington, D.C., September 25, 1977. See Exodus 20:17.

On Ethical Principles
in Government

RESTORATION OF TRUST

I WOULD LIKE to restore the faith of our people in the government because it demonstrates ability and honesty and justice and principles that meet people's needs. I'd like to contribute something, too, to the potential conflict that exists in a free nation between liberty, on the one hand, and equality, on the other. Sometimes they work at cross-purposes. I'd like to try to bring them into correlation. I'd like to have a sense of commitment of our country to the human things that are so important—the family, the community, the individual worth. I'd like to spend our natural resources and financial resources in a better quality of life, not measured by material possessions but by a sense of dedication and a utilization of the talent and ability that God gives us. If I can do those things—more freedom,

[99]

more justice, more equality, a restoration of the principles on which our lives should be based, a trust of people in the government—that would be a notable achievement.

Interview by Pat Robertson, "700 Club," Christian Broadcasting Network, during 1976 campaign

Would you anticipate as president that you would bring godly men into your inner councils or into the cabinet to advise you?

I think it would be a mistake for me to define the qualifications of a public servant according to what kind of a church they attend or what their denomination is. Obviously a commitment to the principles expressed to us by God would be an important prerequisite. I think those are shared by many people who happen not to be Baptists or not to be Christians. The ethical commitments of our lives—unselfishness, truthfulness, honor, a sense of compassion and understanding of other people, a sense of integrity, those principles given to us by God and natural in so many people's lives—would certainly be prerequisites of my selection of anyone to serve in government.

Interview with Pat Robertson, "700 Club," Christian Broadcasting Network, during the 1976 campaign

MORALITY AND FOREIGN POLICY

Does morality apply to basic decisions such as foreign policy?

Yes.

How does it apply?

Well . . . I think that we've made a mistake in our foreign policy in dealing with both strong nations and with nations who are dependent on us for trade advantages—

Can we talk about dictatorships, the morality of liaisons with dictatorships?

Well, I think the moral standards should be encompassed in "do unto others as you would have them do unto you" [paraphrase of Matthew 7:12]. As we have relationships with other governments, I think one of the guiding principles, among others, should be, "what's best for those people who live in the country with which we are dealing?" whether it be Angola or Russia or whether it be the People's Republic of China or whether it be our good friends in Great Britain or China.

If dictatorship be wrong and democracy is right, should the experimental democracies such as ours have relationships with dictatorships that are wrong? Is that the kind of moral judgment you bring to foreign policy?

God says, "Judge not, that ye be not judged" [Matthew 7:1]. Just because I believe in democracy it doesn't mean I think that people who live in countries that might have a different form of government—socialism, communism, fascism, dictatorship, as you expressed it—are wrong. I don't think our country has a prerogative or responsibility to determine the form of government of other people.

We used to be the evangelists of democracy.

Yes, I know. The best way, I think, to induce other people to adopt our own persuasion in democratic principles is to make our own system work.

Interview by John Hart, NBC News, March 28, 1976

BY EXAMPLE, NOT PREACHING

Do you think there's a breakdown of morality that somehow needs to be corrected with the help of the "bully pulpit" of the White House?

I think so.

How would you use that "bully pulpit" to rally for moral values that have been lost?

I wouldn't use it, in spite of Theodore Roosevelt's statement, as a pulpit from which to preach to other people that they're doing wrong. But I would hope by my own example and the statements I make that I could inspire restoration of lost moral values.

You've put a great deal of emphasis on the family and making abortion unnecessary. The reason abortion is necessary, to a large degree, is extramarital sexual relations. You disapprove of that as a Christian?

Yes, I do.

As president, how do you discourage that? By strengthening laws, by enforcing laws that are now not enforced?

No, I don't think so. I don't think the law can have any particular effect there. This is something individuals will have to decide for themselves. I think with my attitude, which I hope will not be condescending, I hope I could influence an adoption of those standards. In almost every faith, religion, there's a prohibition against fornication or adultery. I think it's not acceptable for any sort of measurement of moral standard. I would do everything I could to minimize the need for abortions, which I think are wrong. . . .

Interview by John Hart, NBC News, March 28, 1976

A NEW SPIRIT

IN THIS OUTWARD and physical ceremony, we attest once again to the inner and spiritual strength of our nation. As my high-school teacher, Miss Julia Coleman, used to say, "We must adjust to changing times and still hold to unchanging principles." Here before me is the Bible used in the inauguration of our first president in 1789, and I have just taken the oath of office on the Bible my mother gave me just a few years ago, opened to a timeless admonition from the ancient prophet Michah: "He hath shewed thee, O man, what *is* good; and what doth the LORD require of thee, but to do justly, and to love mercy, and to walk humbly with thy God?" [Micah 6:8]. This inauguration ceremony marks a new beginning, a new dedication within our government, and a new spirit among us all.

Address on inauguration as president, Washington, D.C., January 20, 1977

THE HUMAN RELATIONSHIP

THE HUMAN RELATIONSHIP with God, with our fellow human beings, and with our institutions, is the basis on

[103]

which a democracy is founded. We believe in individuality, and, as one of my favorite philosophers, Kierkegaard, said every person is an individual. Every person is different, with different yearnings, and disappointments, fears, hopes and dreams and aspirations, prejudices, and needs. If we treat people as statistics or as homogeneous bodies, even though we know they're in need, then we will have failed.

To employees of the Department of Health, Education, and Welfare, Washington, D.C., February 16, 1977

On God's Law and
Human Law

OUR PLACE IN GOD'S KINGDOM

THE STRENGTH OF LEADERS can only come from their ability to tap the experience, the judgment, the common sense, the intelligence, the idealism, the hope, the sense of brotherhood and compassion and love, [and] patriotism toward one's country, that exists in the minds and hearts of free men and women everywhere. And those who want to be free. . . .

[In America] different kinds of people with different customs and different dreams and different memories fit together and share our strength toward a high and a common goal. Therein lies the uniqueness of America. And we derive our unique spirit, too, from the common bond that brought us here, a search for human freedom. . . . We need never relinquish our individuality. We need never be ashamed of our heritage but always proud. . . .

What matters is why we came here, and what we do when we come. And what our lives can mean to give our children a greater grasp of the world. A realization of our place in God's kingdom, and a hope that our lives can be meaningful to fellow human beings, who search as we have for a fuller realization of individuality, freedom, liberty, commonality of purpose, an absence of discrimination, truth, justice, honor and equality of opportunity. In what is still, and what I hope will always be, the greatest nation on earth.

Pulaski Day dinner, Chicago, October 10, 1976

RENDER UNTO CAESAR

I DON'T THINK there is any doubt that God wants us to relate personally and aggressively to civil government. In the Old Testament, there are many examples where God confirmed that premise. And, of course, Christ Himself said, "Render unto Caesar the things that are Caesar's; render unto God the things that are God's" [a paraphrase of Matthew 22:21]. We know that Peter and Paul both taught that we should honor civil authority, and we should try to assure that secular law is compatible with God's laws, to obey the government if we agree that there is no conflict with God's commands to us; if there was a conflict, which should be quite rare, that we should obey God's law; that we should be willing to suffer if necessary the consequences of the disobedience of civil law to obey God's will.

On God's Law and Human Law

I also see government as a way to extend ourselves—at least in my own case, I do—and to greatly magnify my own possibility of serving other people, of loving my fellow man, and of dealing with the needs of those who are poor or afflicted or who [have] felt the consequences of discrimination or inequities—so, also, in a governing way, in a protective way, of the security of our country, in alleviating suffering, in following more humane and compassionate feelings of brotherhood and love among people. . . .

Interview by Pat Robertson, "700 Club," Christian Broadcasting Network, during the 1976 campaign

Playboy: *We're confused. You say morality can't be legislated, yet you support certain laws because they preserve old moral standards. How do you reconcile the two positions?*

Carter: I believe people should honor civil laws. If there is a conflict between God's law and civil law, we should honor God's law. But we should be willing to accept civil punishment. Most of Christ's original followers were killed because of their belief in Christ; they violated the civil law in following God's law. Reinhold Niebuhr, a theologian who has dealt with this problem at length, says that the framework of law is a balancing of forces in a society; the law itself tends to alleviate tensions brought about by these forces. . . .

Interview by Robert Scheer, *Playboy*, November 1976. Copyright © 1976 by *Playboy*.

A HIGHER AUTHORITY

What do you feel is the basic responsibility of the state?

Well, we have had from the very beginning of our nation a dependence upon religious faith as part of our political framework. The Constitution, the Declaration of Independence, our laws, our coins, "In God We Trust," ". . . One Nation under God indivisible . . ." This has, I think, caused us in moments of strife, moments of uncertainty, moments of crisis, to look for a higher authority than man's laws for the proper relationship between people in our nation and also between our nation and other nations. And these are ethical principles that are common to many relationships—compassion, brotherhood, love, truth, honesty, decency—those kinds of things are always tenets of religious faith to which our nation can go back. . . .

Interview by Ralph Blodgett, *Liberty*, September–October 1976

ON GOD'S UNCHANGING LAW

GOD'S LAW DOESN'T CHANGE, no matter if one is in Plains, Georgia, Washington, the Soviet Union, China, or Paki-

stan. Congress meets and goes home. God's law doesn't change.

Couples' Class, First Baptist Church, Washington, D.C., February 20, 1977. This was the first time Carter taught Sunday school here after transferring his family's membership from the Plains Baptist Church. The lesson was about the rich young man who went away brokenhearted when Jesus told him, "take up the cross, and follow me" (Mark 10:17–22).

Playboy: *We'd like to ask you a blunt question: Isn't it just these views about what's "sinful" and what's "immoral" that contribute to the feeling that you might get a call from God, or get inspired and push the wrong button? More realistically, wouldn't we expect a puritanical tone to be set in the White House if you're elected?*

Carter: Harry Truman was a Baptist. Some people get very abusive about the Baptist faith. If people want to know about it, they can read the New Testament. The main thing is that we don't think we're better than anyone else. We are taught not to judge other people. But as to some of the behavior you've mentioned, I can't change the teachings of Christ. I can't change the teachings of Christ! I believe in them, and a lot of people in this country do as well. . . .

Interview by Robert Scheer, *Playboy*, November 1976.
Copyright © 1976 by *Playboy*.

Religion and Politics

In what way has being a born-again Christian affected your role as the president?

There was a great deal of doubt in the country when I began my campaign because I am a devout Christian. I have never found that this interfered with my performance of duties as a governor or as a candidate or as president of our country. I recognize very clearly the prohibition in the Constitution about an unwarranted intrusion of the state or the government into religion or vice versa. I worship daily; the last thing I do every evening is to have a private worship service with my wife. We never fail to do this; I pray frequently during the day; I seek God's guidance. I don't try to use the power and prestige of my office to cause other people to adopt the same faith that I happen to have. I don't think this is contrary to the hopes or the expressed beliefs of our Founding Fathers. In the constitution of the United States, we recognize God as the guiding leader of us all. We leave people a right to either worship Him, or not to worship, whatever form of God they choose. But I found it very beneficial to me to have something in my life that never changes. In the face of constantly changing political and military and economic circumstances, my religious faith doesn't change. It is a stabilizing factor in my life. It binds me closer to the members of my family, it gives us something in common. I believe and hope that our nation's deep belief in God will be a stabilizing factor in generations ahead.

Senior High School Forum, Nashua, New Hampshire,
February 18, 1978. The question was asked by John Bryant
of Cornid High School.

WORSHIP GOD, NOT FREEDOM

IN MANY WAYS, the American people almost worship the concept of freedom and liberty. We believe man should not be dominated by the government. Freedom is a word that means an awful lot to us. . . . It's a mistake for Americans to worship freedom or liberty or individuality or any word like that. We worship God. God is love.

> Men's Bible Class, Plains Baptist Church, December 12, 1976

A LIFE SHAPED BY COMMITMENT TO CHRIST

Can you give me one example of a way in which your religious convictions have shaped your political actions and an example of an instance in which you set aside your own personal religious convictions?

My own religious convictions on the abortion issue are in conflict with the laws that our nation must observe. . . . I favored the very strict abortion law Georgia had originally had but, after the Supreme Court ruled, as governor of the state it was mandatory that I comply with the ruling. That is one instance where my own beliefs were in conflict with the laws of our country. I try to utilize my own religious beliefs as a constant guide in making deci-

[111]

sions as a private or public citizen. We had court reform to provide better equity in the court. We have initiated complete prison reform to give more compassionate attention to the needs of Georgia people. We have instituted treatment programs for alcoholics and drug addicts, for mentally retarded children. All of those I consider to be poor, deprived, despised, unfortunate, illiterate, afflicted, who belong to a group against which there is discrimination, ought to be the prime responsibility of me as a powerful, influential public servant. . . . If I tried to ascribe that completely to religious convictions if would probably be inappropriate, but my life has been shaped in the church, by my deep commitment as a Christian, and my own knowledge of the example of the life of Christ and the observation, through my own religious learning, of the attitude of Christ toward other human beings. This has been obviously an example that I followed.

Interview by Jim Castelli, Catholic National News Service, August 9, 1976

SHAPING GOVERNMENT TO THE WORD OF GOD

WE HAVE A RESPONSIBILITY to try to shape government so that it does exemplify the teaching of God. . . .

To reporters at Plains Baptist Church, June 27, 1976

A LITTLE PIECE OF GOD'S KINGDOM

GOD'S KINGDOM is not remote, on top of a white cloud. Christ said God's kingdom can be around the Christian. There's a little bit, a piece of God's kingdom, and we're in the middle of it. "Thy Kingdom come." There's only one way God's kingdom can come on earth, and that's through us. We're kind of proud; we're the epitome of the evangelistic, well-organized, rich, the affluent. We must spread God's kingdom by the influence of your life and my life. Or do you hope other Christians will do the things you or I don't do?

> Couples' Class, First Baptist Church, Washington, D.C., April 24, 1977 *

*For text of lesson, see pages 178–187.

On the Compatibility of Faith and Public Service

A REPORTER OR PEANUT FARMER AND GOD

THERE IS NO INCOMPATIBILITY between the life of a reporter and the life of a peanut farmer or any other profession and a life dedicated to God. The Christian faith gives us a chance to magnify our presence.

> Men's Bible Class, Plains Baptist Church, August 29, 1976. The lesson was on Christian unity, "In Mission Together," drawn from I Corinthians. The young church at Corinth had been torn by dissension. Some members claimed loyalty to Paul, others to Apollo, others to Peter. Carter said the spiritual mission of the church should override denominational disputes.

On the Compatibility of Faith and Public Service

I'VE NEVER SEEN any conflict between being a deeply committed Christian on the one hand and holding public office on the other.

> African Methodist Episcopal Zion Church, Buffalo, New York, March 21, 1976

I HAVE NEVER DETECTED nor experienced any conflict between God's will and my political duty. It is obvious that when I violate one, at the same time I violate the other.

> Southern Baptist Brotherhood Commission, Atlanta, Georgia, June 16, 1978

I'VE BEEN A CHRISTIAN, I've also been on the school board during the tough integration years, I've been a state senator two terms, I've been a governor four years. I've never seen any incompatibility between those two parts of my life. I've never let my religious convictions orient my decisions on a political matter and never have tried to use the strength of my political office to force my religious convictions on somebody else.

> Interview by Ralph Blodgett, *Liberty*, September–October 1976

STRIVING FOR PERFECTION

I THINK the biblical moral standards are compatible with the laws of our country. In most instances in a nation like ours, the original concepts of the law have been derived from our ancestors and they are compatible with the Ten Commandments and the interpretation of the Ten Commandments as expressed by Christ. This is something that a president can do, by a rigid insistence on adherence to the law and by one's own personal example.

I think to the extent that a president or anyone else claims to be perfect and asks other people to emulate one's own holiness that's possibly counterproductive. I know that Christ teaches and the Bible teaches throughout that all of us are sinful, that we come short of the glory of God, that the wages of sin are death, that God loves us, that He sent His Son to be our Saviour, if we believe in Christ we can have eternal life. Christ in many ways admonishes us against self-pride, against the condemnation of others, when we have within ourselves sinfulness as well. This is the kind of attitude that I would try to adopt as president.

Along with the belief in Christ comes an obligation to abide by God's laws, recognizing that we can't be perfect, but we ought to strive for perfection. . . . That constant searching to be better as a nation, as a human being, as a political leader is part of my hope for the future.

Interview with National Religious Broadcasters,
Indianapolis, Indiana, October 14, 1976

A SINGLE STANDARD

Columnist Joseph Kraft said in March, "Is America ready for a Christian president from the South? . . . But the crowning asset is Mr. Carter's glowing personal faith, his unblushing and repeatedly articulated belief in God and family and trust and love and charity. That religious quality is what sets Mr. Carter apart from all other Democratic candidates." How has God manifested Himself in your life and what would your own personal relationship with Christ mean if you become president?

My deep and consistent religious faith is . . . the most important thing in my life. . . . It's something I have not injected into the election campaign, but it has become important to the news media. After a great deal of prayerful thought I decided I ought not to conceal it, not to disavow it, and not to use it to get votes. I think I'll be a better president because of my deep religious convictions. I think I was a better governor because I had deep faith in God. . . .

There is no incompatibility, in my opinion, between a person's deep religious beliefs, no matter what they might be, and public service. I'm a Baptist and I believe very strongly in the separation of church and state. I don't believe that we should use our religion to orient government programs. I don't think we ought to use the government to try to change anybody's religious beliefs. That's guaranteed under the Constitution and I have a very deep commitment to that.

As we make decisions about people's lives our deep convictions can be a guide on how to treat people decently, to bring peace in the world, to understand suffering, to be fair, to tell the truth. These kinds of characteristics of a human being—they are admirable—ought to be the characteristics of the government of free human beings. For too long now we've had a different standard of ethics, of morality, of honesty and truthfulness toward government and politics than we have had in our own lives. I'd like to exemplify as president, I hope in a humble way and a constantly searching way, the kind of life I would like to live as a member of a church or as a Christian. And I don't believe I'll be a worse president because of it.

Response to a question asked by Cal Thomas of KPRC-TV News, Houston, April 20, 1976

I DO NEED your continued friendship and support, your open criticism when I make mistakes, and your constant prayers that the judgments that I make will be compatible with our highest commitments, our highest faith, our highest beliefs. We have a chance to make our country greater than in the past. But it depends not on the identity of the president, but on the common trust and strength of our people. I am one of you, and you are a part of me. That realization gives me a quiet comfort that I can serve in such a way as not to embarrass you. . . . We Baptists feel that we have an obligation to our country to devote our lives to the furtherance of its finest ideals and commitments. We also have an opportunity to serve our government and to try to elevate those standards to meet the standards set for us by Jesus Christ. I don't see any incompatibility there.

To the trustees of the Brotherhood Commission of the Southern Baptist Convention, White House Rose Garden, May 13, 1977. Carter served as a trustee for six years until his resignation after election as president.

SEARCH FOR DIVINE GUIDANCE

Let me welcome you not only as the President of the United States but as an eminent American Baptist. I am a Baptist myself. . . . I would like to express my gladness that you have been elected to the post of the president of the United States, as a man, as a believer who is not ashamed of it and of his evangelical convictions. . . . We all know that you are a practicing Christian, as every Baptist should be—as every good Baptist should be. And I would like to ask whether your religious convictions help you in executing the job of president of such a big country. Can you quote an example in how the evangelical principles helped you in solving any complicated problem?

My own religious convictions are deep and personal. I seek divine guidance when I make a difficult decision as president and also am supported, of course, by a common purpose which binds Christians together in a belief in the human dignity of mankind and in the search for worldwide peace—recognizing, of course, that those who don't share my faith quite often have the same desires and hopes.

My own constant hope is that all nations would give

maximum freedom of religion and freedom of expression
to their people, and I will do all I can within the bounds of
propriety to bring that hope into realization.

> Response to query by Polish journalist, news conference,
> Warsaw, Poland, December 30, 1977

I HOPE THAT ALL OF YOU will make a special promise to
yourselves during this holiday season to pray for guidance
in our lives' purposes, guidance for wisdom and commitment and honesty of public officials and other leaders,
guidance that we can see our nation realize its great potential and the vision that formed it two hundred years ago,
and guidance that we will fulfill our deepest moral and
religious commitments.

> The lighting of the national Christmas tree, December 15,
> 1977

REPENTANCE IS PERSONAL

*In the Old Testament it mentions many times where God has
called the nation to repentance for their immoral actions. . . . If
you are in a position to do this before the American people and
before God, would you do it?*

My own religious faith is one that is much more personal. I feel that we have a direct access to God through
prayer and that repentance is a personal thing. I don't

believe that it is my responsibility to repent before God for what our nation has done in the past or may do even while I am in the White House. I think that is something that has to be initiated and carried out by individual Americans. Obviously, if I see a sinful act or an improper or heartless act being carried out by our nation in the past or present or future, it is my responsibility as president to stop that action and to atone through action for inequities or suffering that has been caused by it . . .

I don't consider myself to be the spiritual leader of this country. But I am the political leader. I have a right, I think, and a duty, to be frank with the American people about my own belief; and I am not a priest nor a bishop, nor someone who fills a religious pulpit and is authorized nor asked to repent for the whole country. I have answered your question in a fumbling way. But that is the way I feel about it. I recognize my own personal shortcomings and sinfulness. I do ask God to forgive me. I try to do better and I think the American people, whether they are religious or not, have the same strong inclination to correct deficiencies, to repair wrongs, to turn ourselves in a much closer way personally and collectively to exemplify the highest possible moral principles on which our nation has been so great.

Senior High School Forum, Nashua, New Hampshire, February 18, 1978. The question was asked by Bruce Pravot of Hillsboro Deering High School.

On Power as Servanthood

SERVANT, NOT MASTER

WE LEARNED AS PLANNERS to assume the role of servants
and not masters.

> *Why Not the Best?* 1975, p. 99. Carter refers to his role in an
> eight-county planning and development commission in
> Georgia before he ran for governor a second time in 1970.

THE ATTITUDE OF A SERVANT

A GREAT, STRONG, SURE PERSON need not prove it always.
That's the way it is with Christ. And that's the way it is
with Christians. When you're sure of your strength, you
can exhibit compassion, emotion, love, concern, equal-

ity—and, even better than equality, the attitude of a servant. You can say, "I'm not only better than you, you're
better than I am. And I want to work with you."

Men's Bible Class, Plains Baptist Church, July 18, 1976.
This was three days after Carter won his party's
nomination for president.*

FIRST, AND PUBLIC SERVANT

I NEED YOU to help me. We're all in it together. I'm no better than any of you. I recognize that I ought to be not
First Boss but First Servant.

To employees of the Department of Health, Education and
Welfare, Washington, D.C., February 16, 1977

WHEN THE DISCIPLES struggled among themselves for superiority in God's eyes, Jesus said, "Whosoever would be
chief among you, let him be His servant." And although
we use the phrase—sometimes glibly—"public servant,"
it's hard for us to translate the concept of a president of
the United States into genuine servant.

National Prayer Breakfast, Washington, January 27, 1977.
Carter was paraphrasing Matthew 20:27.

*For text of lesson, see pages 162–175.

SETTING AN EXAMPLE

The Declaration of Independence speaks about man being equal and free to pursue happiness. Has there been a switch where our people expect government to provide happiness for them?

When they expect that, people are disappointed. The law is important and government is important. But you can't derive fulfillment or happiness or a sense of justice or brotherhood or compassion from the law. There are institutions that are much older that are much more important, for instance, the church, the family, and the community. One of the reasons we've come to rely much more heavily on government to provide their needs is because of the destruction of the relationships within the family or the church. . . .

Do you do that through moral persuasion and leadership more than through passage of legislation?

I think both. . . . The other thing is for the president to set an example, not only himself but members of his family, the family of the vice president, the cabinet appointments, public statements about the precious nature of the relationship of human beings who are close by blood ties or by common religion or by common social conviction. Those things ought to be preserved. I think we've had too much destruction of it because of lack of attention given to those important needs in government.

> Interview by Pat Robertson, "700 Club," Christian Broadcasting Network, during the 1976 campaign

On Power as Servanthood

Your position as a Christian was probably a very major element in your winning campaign. I am curious what you think the government's responsibility to the spiritual and moral development of its people should be? What do you think it is? And since you have been president, how have you tried to meet that responsibility? I think this is a very pertinent question to the youth here because in our times there [are many] misleading forces in the world.

I think if there is one group in our nation who is the most alienated and disillusioned when public officials do not exemplify decency and morality and humanity and sensitivity and compassion, it is young people. You have been in the forefront, you and others who are now older who were your age, of trying to restore morality to our country. . . . When we were struggling . . . to give black people and other minority groups equal treatment under the Constitution—the simple right to vote, to go to school, to have a job, to own a home—young people . . . were courageous enough to endanger their physical health, or even lives, to strive for an unpopular cause. When our nation was involved in the war in Vietnam, the ones who first spoke out and said "This is a war that is not compatible with the principles of America" were young people. At first it was a tiny group. Then it grew and grew . . . and eventually the older people, the parents said, "Well, maybe my child is right." And ultimately we withdrew from Vietnam because of the influence of young people demanding that our country stand for the same principles on which it was founded and which made it great.

I sensed as I campaigned throughout this country for two years that there was a frustrated feeling and a sense of despair and even embarrassment about some of the things that had been happening in Washington: The Watergate revelations, the breakdown in compatibility and partnership between the president and the congress, the constant blaming of one another for mistakes honestly made, the revelations about illegalities in the CIA and involvement in the Vietnam war as well. And I believe that we felt that, on an international basis, our country had abandoned those principles. We espoused any sort of totalitarian dictatorship if it furthered our own interests temporarily. . . . And we forgot about trying to spread what we stand for among the other nations of the world.

In my own acceptance speech at the Democratic National Convention and in my inauguration speech I promised the American people that when I was president the principle of human rights would again be raised as a banner behind which American people could rally and of which American people would again be proud. This is what we have tried to do. It is a difficult and sensitive issue; it is easy to say you are for human rights, but it is difficult to force other nations over whom you have no control to honor the principles of human rights. We have made very good progress. . . .

I don't believe there is a single leader in a country in the world who doesn't think frequently or even constantly, about the question of human rights: How is the world going to judge me in how I treat the citizens who are ruled by my administration? We have made good progress already. But I think the restoration of that decency and common sense and humanity and morality to our own government is the only thing that can hold us together.

And when you think back through history, even the most unpopular presidents now are the ones identified as the greatest. They were the ones that made difficult decisions, based on the principles of religion. Abraham Lincoln was probably excoriated or criticized most by the press of almost any president who ever served. He did what he thought was right. Harry Truman's popularity went down to 23 percent, the lowest any president has ever had. But he did it because he thought it was right to begin giving black people a chance to have equal treatment in the armed forces, not popular in the South. He wanted to restore Europe with a great financial aid that came from the taxpayers' pockets in this country, not a popular thing at all. He gave aid to Turkey and Greece. He organized the United Nations. And now I think it is generally accepted that Harry Truman is one of our great presidents.

I don't consider that they were great because of something within them, and the same thing applies to me. But I think the greatness comes from accurately exemplifying in the White House the highest principles of the American people. And the demands that you make as young people in government will help to restore those standards, make them more rigid and more demanding. Whether an incumbent officeholder is mayor or governor or senator or president, Democratic or Republican, you ought to demand the utmost in ethics, integrity, and morality from them. If they don't measure up to your standards, I hope you work as hard as you can to put somebody else in the office.

> Senior High School Forum, Nashua, New Hampshire, February 18, 1978. The question was asked by Keith White of Manchester West High School.

PRIVATE RESPONSIBILITY

To THE EXTENT that we can distinguish between potentially productive social service recipients and those who are permanently and inherently dependent on government services, we can minister effectively to both groups. This is the first step toward the development of an acceptable welfare and public health system, and it certainly is within the capability of the American people. We should not underestimate the personal ability and obligation of private citizens to minister to those who are in need. There has been an excessive inclination to wash our hands of this responsibility, and to assume the government alone can deal with the problems of the poor and the afflicted.

Why Not the Best? 1975, p. 132.

WE ARE PARTNERS in a process. . . . I don't want any of you to be afraid of change, because I hope, working closely with you, to bring about a structure of government—the evolution of regulations and policies and guidelines and purposes and instructions and an organizational setup—to make your one life, like mine, which is very valuable in the eyes of God, be meaningful, because each career represented here can be fruitful or it can be wasted.

Remarks to employees of the Department of Labor, Washington, D.C., February 9, 1977

HOLD UP MY ARMS

WE LEARNED from the Bible about the fallibilities of people who were given great responsibility. I remember the story

of the escape of the Israelites from Egypt when Moses was
a man appointed by God to lead [Exodus 17]. And when
the Israelites were in a battle, God told Moses, "Hold up
your arm." And as long as Moses held up his arm, the
Israelites won. But after an hour or two or three, his arm
got weary and it began to sink and the Israelites began to
lose. His brother Aaron went and propped up his arm for
a while. And later on Hur propped up Moses' arm for a
while; and the Israelites won. Well, I don't under any circumstances equate myself with Moses. But I would like to
remind you of this: You elected me to be president. You
gave me a job to do.

> At "Southern Salute to the President," a Democratic
> fund-raising dinner, Atlanta, Georgia, January 20, 1978

ON NOT DISAPPOINTING THE PEOPLE

I PRAY GOD that, with your help, you'll never be disappointed that I am in the White House. I need your help,
your encouragement, your advice, your sound judgment,
and your prayers.

> On arriving at Allen C. Thompson Airport, Jackson,
> Mississippi, July 21, 1977

TO MEET THE PEOPLE'S DREAMS

ONE OF THE CONSTANT FEARS I have is that I will act in a
way as president that is incompatible with and contrary to

[129]

the concerns and hopes and dreams and aspirations of the American people. . . .

Senior High School Forum, Nashua, New Hampshire, February 18, 1978

In the early days of the campaign, you made a prayer breakfast speech in Miami on the theme of God and country. I think the promise you gave the electorate was helpful in winning the election. Do you feel, since you are now in office, you have fulfilled your goals in this respect?

No. And I don't know whether to answer that as a politician or a Christian. As a Christian, you know, I realized that I am sinful, that I fall short of the expectations of God and my fellow human beings; and as a politician, I know that there are many times when either I or my associates have disappointed the American people, no matter how hard we try.

I think that there has been a restoration, . . . in some areas of government, of the American people's trust. . . . I felt during the campaign, and I feel now, that the American consciousness was dealt a very severe blow by the Vietnam war and by the Watergate revelations and by the violations of law that were proven against the CIA. I felt as an individual and as a potential president that the people were embarrassed about their own government and felt that the nation and its image was not as high as it had been in the past, as it was originally conceived or as the American people expected it to be.

And we have tried to improve that image, not by misleading anybody, but by trying to stand for things that we felt were important. Human rights, in its broadest definition, is one of the notable elements in that effort. We have had a concerted commitment to bring peace to some of the troubled areas of the world and we have tried genuinely to understand the special attitudes of billions of people, literally, who in the past had condemned the United States and what we stood for. I think we are competing adequately with the communist nations for the hearts and souls and trust and friendship, and, to be more practical, the trade and political alignments with nations that in the past were either non-committed at best, or oriented toward totalitarian atheistic philosophies at worst. I think we have made some progress there.

But I can't say we have done an adequate job. There is a lot of inertia and we make a lot of mistakes. But we are trying hard and I think we are making some progress.

To out-of-town editors, the White House,
July 28, 1978

On the Biblical Injunction of Peace

ON GOD'S BOUNTY

To put the people of the world back to work, to discourage a rampant robbing of people by inflation, to share the proper and fair use of raw materials and other supplies that come from the less-developed countries, and to share with those less fortunate nations the bounties that God has given the world. . . .

On goals of discussions of the International Economic Summit in London, May 5, 1977

We have a tremendous reservoir of inherent strength in our country over which you have authority and for which you have a measure of responsibility. That is the open farmland, fields, and forests that God has given us. I want to be sure they are used for peace and for humanitarian reasons and for the welfare of all the people in future years.

To employees of the Department of Agriculture, Washington, D.C., February 16, 1977

AND CONCENTRATED within your own department here is a focusing of inherent, very difficult questions that must be addressed now and in the future: how to preserve and still use the precious resources with which our nation has been blessed. . . .

To employees of the Department of the Interior, February 18, 1977

GOD HAS BLESSED US with tremendous natural resources.

Interview with four television networks, the White House, December 28, 1977

RELIGIOUS INFLUENCE UPON HISTORY

I was fascinated on that Sunday morning when Mr. Sadat and Mr. Begin took the whole world into its Sunday school room and

[133]

it occurred to me then, knowing I was going to see you at the end of the year, to ask you whether in your philosophy you believe there is a religious influence upon history?

Yes, I went to my own church early that morning and for the first time here gave a public prayer, although that is a common thing in Plains. And the thrust of my comment to the press afterward was that I have found that one of the common things that Begin and Sadat and I share is a deep religious conviction. They mention it frequently; so did Crown Prince Fahd [of Saudi Arabia] when he was here. President Assad [of Syria], Begin and Sadat frequently refer to it publicly. So do I. I think the fact that we worship the same God and are bound by basically the same moral principles is a possible source for resolution of differences. I was always convinced that if Sadat and Begin could get together, they would be bound by that common belief.

Interview by James Reston on December 1, 1977,
published in *The New York Times*, December 5, 1977

A PRAYER FOR PEACE

O FATHER in heaven, the people of Thy world want peace. Your Son, our Saviour, Jesus Christ, was the Prince of Peace. There rarely has been an opportunity in the history of our mankind when the hearts and minds of people of all nations could be attuned to common hope in a simultaneous moment of thanksgiving, and concern, and prayer.

We are especially concerned and hopeful about the Middle East of the people of Lebanon, and Syria, and Jordan, Egypt and Israel, who have been constantly torn, and killed each other in a continuing stream of conflicts, both large and small—four wars in the last thirty years—while the people have suffered torment and frustration, all desiring to live in peace, all suffering from the ravages of war.

This morning, God our Father in heaven, we have perhaps a more vivid realization that, in spite of the yearnings of the people for peace in the Middle East, chosen leaders have not responded adequately to this constant yearning. Yesterday the Prime Minister of Israel worshiped you in a Jewish temple and, later, the President of Egypt worshiped you in a Moslem mosque and then, today, we worship you in a Christian holy place. We remember our Saviour was crucified and buried, and people all over the world are worshiping you today in the genuine hope that the meaning of these historic interviews might bring a new realization of the common commitment which binds us all together, in spite of the national boundaries and in spite of the fear. We pray for peace in Your Name.

No one can predict the outcome of this historic meeting taking place this weekend, but we know it is in Your Name. I know Prime Minister Begin to be an honorable and deeply religious man. He prays for me that we might truly lead our people in Your desire, in Your Name, toward peace. I know President Sadat to be an honorable and courageous man. He has pledged to pray for me and I have pledged to pray for him. As we open our hearts may they provide an avenue to bind us all together. Be with us leaders and all other leaders that Thy people may be nurtured by these common dreams and strengthened by our organization. With Your guidance it is possible that peace might come to Your Glory.

Public prayer, Special Service for Peace, First Baptist Church, Washington, D.C., November 20, 1977

THE OBSTACLES MAN CREATES

You see the hand of God moving in all of this, don't you?

I think the fact that the Arabs, the Moslems, the Jews, the Christians all worship the same God, and freely acknowledge it, is a binding force that gives an avenue of communication and common purpose.

I know that when Crown Prince Fahd was here, he talked about this to the members of congress and to me, and it's mentioned frequently by leaders like Prime Minister Begin and President Sadat when they talk to me privately, that we do have this common religious bond that at least provides a possible avenue for peace if we can remove the obstacles that men create.

So, yes, I do see it as a common bond.

Exchange with reporters outside First Baptist Church, Washington, D.C., November 20, 1977

What do you think about the Bible prophecy in Isaiah 19:23–24 apparently being fulfilled in our times, when Egypt and Syria will align themselves with Israel in the last days?

On the Biblical Injunction of Peace

I believe that one of the great positive factors in eventually finding a resolution of the differences in the Middle East is the deep religious conviction of both Prime Minister Begin and President Sadat. They and we as Christians worship the same God. Our religious beliefs differ in some degree. But there is a special interrelationship between the Arabs in Egypt and the Jews in Israel. They recognize Abraham as a common father of them all. I think they understand, as you say, the prophesy in Isaiah, as applying to both peoples, that peace between Egypt and Israel is foreordained by God and that they play a role in carrying out God's purposes.

Senior High School Forum, Nashua, New Hampshire, February 18, 1978. The question was asked by John Bryant of Cornid High School.

PEACE, FINALLY

WITH ALL THE DIFFICULTIES, all the conflicts, I believe that our planet must finally obey the biblical injunction to "follow after the things which make for peace."

Address to the 31st annual Southern Legislative Conference, Charleston, South Carolina, July 21, 1977. Carter was quoting from Romans 14:19.

PEACEMAKERS

THERE IS NO NOBLER CALLING on this earth than the seeking for peace. For it is that reason which caused the Bible to say that peacemakers shall be called the sons of God.

> At the departure of Egyptian President Anwar Sadat, the White House, February 8, 1978. Carter referred to Matthew 5:9, the Revised Standard Version. The King James translation refers to "the children of God."

IV. The Reach of the Church

On Church and State

ON REQUIRING WORSHIP OF GOD

WE MET IN SPECIAL SESSION in the summer of 1974 in the Georgia Senate, and worked industriously to evolve a model document as the fundamental organic law of Georgia. The first shock was when we could not pass the basic bill of rights, guaranteeing freedom from search and freedom of religion. A requirement that God be worshiped was passed by the Senate, and a few years later my vote against this requirement, and for the U.S. Constitution language, was used against me as "proof" that I was an atheist!

Why Not the Best? 1975, p. 89.

I DON'T THINK that any person should be forced to pray at a certain time or pray in a certain fashion in the public schools. I think private prayer should be permitted, but to require prayer I don't approve, and I think that the court rulings on that subject are proper.

Interview by Jim Castelli, Catholic News Service August 9, 1976

On Commitment

THE CHURCH'S MISSION

THE TEST OF A CHURCH is not in its building or in its staff, but in the number of people reached for Christ.

> White House luncheon for ten Southern Baptist leaders, June 7, 1977

*

YOU'RE ESTABLISHING several new churches, very good. That's a good evangelism program. I think St. Mark would have been pleased.

> To his Holiness Pope Shenuda III of the Coptic Christians at the White House, April 20, 1977. According to tradition and scripture, the apostle Peter established the church at Rome, now the Roman Catholic Church, and the Apostle

Mark founded the Coptic Church in Egypt where there are
now seven million Coptic Christians. Shenuda III is the
117th Pope to follow Mark.

Paul was a man who did not believe in a split-level
church because Christ also had not believed in a split-level
church. Sometimes even in our modern day we think
there are different kinds of Christians—maybe white
Christians are better than black Christians; Southern
Christians are better than Northern Christians; Christians
in a small, stable community are better than Christians in
transient, larger, impersonal churches. That is not the
way the church is. It's not the way Christ taught.

Men's Bible Class, Plains Baptist Church, June 20, 1976*

A SOUND DOCTRINE

THE PURPOSE OF THE CHURCH is to preserve and teach a
sound doctrine, based on the unique part of the Christian
faith, a living Christ, God and our brother distant to be
revered and feared; close to be loved, to set a pattern for
our lives, to shape our lives. A sound doctrine is the gospel of saving grace.

Couples' Class, First Baptist Church, Washington, D.C.,
April 24, 1977†

*For text of lesson, see pages 156–162.
† For text of lesson, see pages 178–187.

What is the doctrine of the Christian faith? Jesus came forth as the Son of God. For what purpose? To save sinners. Faith is union with the living Christ. The reason Christ came to earth was to save sinners. Like them? Like us. That's why the Baptists don't have a creed. We have a faith . . . the living God, the living Christ, loves us. It's simple. God is love, personal and demanding, demanding. Did Paul tell Timothy to sit on your cushion at home, a good boy, and enjoy the blessing and knowledge of Christ, stay away from wicked people? No. That's false doctrine.

Couples' Class, First Baptist Church, Washington, D.C., April 24, 1977*

OUR FOREMOST COMMITMENT

IF SOMEONE ASKED US to list in order of priority the things most important in our lives, I'm sure we would immediately say, "My country"; I'm sure we would also say, "My family"; I'm sure we'd also say, "My own reputation as a decent human being." But my guess is that after we gave careful thought and consideration of the eternal placement of our lives we would say that our foremost commitment is to God, to Christ our Saviour, and there would not be any doubt in our mind about it. . . . When I sought public office I made an effort, along with members of my family, that I never would have dreamed possible before. Day and night, total commitment . . . for months and months, leaving my home, facing the most

*For text of lesson, see pages 178–187.

uncertain of all futures, placing my strong convictions and dreams in the hands of hundreds of thousands, even millions, of people whom I had never known and never met. . . . In your own lives the highest demands were made upon you and you were able to reach for strength and commitment and dedication and ability that you didn't know was there. . . .

Many of us have pretty much of an inclination to look around us, to observe with great gratification our own blessings, our physical belongings, . . . the social prestige we enjoy in our own communities, the admiration we sometimes acquire from regular church service or even from a dedicated life in the church, and we say, "We have need of this according to our own merit and deserts."

[But] the great commission of all of us is to carry the good news, God's news, throughout the world. . . . When we compare what we could do, when we plumb the depths of our souls and make a total commitment to that effort [we find that] our progress has been mediocre at best. . . . I've lived now for fifty-three years, and, I would say, three different weeks in my life of fifty-three years have been devoted without interference to the service of Christ. It's a very small contribution for someone who has been blessed with time to spare, superior educational opportunities, and the financial resources that give me the freedom to do infinitely more. . . . I think there must be some of you that share that confession with me.

We have an opportunity now to bring about a resurgence of that commitment, the renewal of the meaning of the great commission, and to be, in effect, pioneers in trying to inspire others who look to us for leadership to contribute their own lives and their own work, without sacrifices, really, to furthering the kingdom of Christ. I think, in the process, we would reach the height of fulfillment, of appreciation of a new relationship with God, a binding together, in a spirit of brotherhood and sisterhood, of those about us that, perhaps, would be almost unprecedented. . . . Christ only had twelve disciples—eleven survived—and their influence spread throughout the world.

I wish, in a way, that I was free to do more. After my service in my present office, I intend to do more. . . . I [speak] in gratitude as a fellow Christian who loves my Saviour to implore you to listen to the descriptions of others who "follow me . . ."

I consider myself to be your brother. I know I benefit from your . . . constant prayers. You will be remembered in mine. And, together, I believe, we can make this a turning point in . . . a single Christian life, a single church, a single denomination in God's kingdom here on earth.

> To the Missionary Service Corps, Southern Baptist Convention, Washington, D.C., May 2, 1978

A COMMON SPIRIT

TWO THOUSAND YEARS AGO—or twenty-one hundred years ago—the Maccabees fought for and achieved a tremendous victory for freedom. This was the first occurrence in the history of humankind when the basic struggle was for religious freedom. And that was a precursor of the constant struggle for the Jewish people to have their own land, free of outside domination, a chance to live in peace, to wor-

ship God as they please. . . . and I hope that this ceremony will remind all the world that Israel and the United
States, we, stand together in a spirit of deep commitment,
with a common religious background and with a common
commitment to peace and a recognition of the great
courage that was required more than two centuries ago
and which is still required to achieve and maintain that
difficult goal of peace, and, also, freedom, together.

> On receiving the Hanukkah torch from representatives of
> Masada, the Zionist Youth Organization, December 7,
> 1977. Judah the Maccabee succeeded in recapturing
> Jerusalem from the Syrian ruler Antiochus Epiphanes in
> 165 B.C.

As you solemnly review and judge your own conduct
during the past year, we are all reminded that we serve
God most faithfully by showing concern for our friends
and neighbors.

In a world made small by modern technology, all peoples and nations have become closer together, and the concern for others has become more important than ever.
This is the wellspring of our nation's commitment to
human rights, and it is why we are determined that all of
America's words and deeds will honor that commitment.

Among the Rosh Hashanah prayers recited in the synagogue is one which looks toward the day when mankind
will be joined in universal brotherhood. This is a prayer to
which all of us add our heartfelt "amen" as we wish each
of you a happy and prosperous New Year.

> At Rosh Hashanah, August 15, 1977

On Commitment

CHRISTMAS HAS A SPECIAL MEANING for those of us who are Christians, those of us who believe in Christ, those of us who know that almost two thousand years ago, the Son of Peace was born, to give us a vision of perfection, a vision of humility, a vision of unselfishness, a vision of compassion, a vision of love.

Lighting of the national Christmas tree, December 15, 1977

IN A CIVILIZATION marred by disputes and conflicts, the ministers of God, representing all faiths, help lead the human family to an understanding of His love and His peace. Clergymen of all denominations point the way to a richer, more fulfilling life through higher moral standards. The clergy inspire all of us to hold firm to what is right—against what is wrong. They call upon us to practice charity and compassion. They bring us together and nearer to our Creator.

Proclamation of International Clergy Week, January 28, 1977

V. Teaching and Preaching

The Teaching Mission

LIVE AS THOUGH CHRIST IS COMING

The Bible teaches that Jesus will come a second time in an unexpected, unusual moment. The study of the final days—eschatology—was the lesson topic at the Men's Class in the Plains Baptist Church a few days after Carter had spoken out publicly in detail about his faith for the first time during the 1976 campaign. His text was Matthew 24.

Last Sunday we saw that the Pharisees were asking Christ questions, trying to trip Him up. He challenged them and told them they were a generation of vipers who ignored the general teachings of God [Matthew 23]. This was the last week before He died. After that encounter with the Pharisees there was no doubt in the mind of His disciples that He was going to be crucified.

The last Tuesday of His life He went into the temple . . . Rosalynn and I have been in Old Jerusalem. We were there three or four days and we would get up at daybreak and walk in the Old City with maps and try and figure out where the different places were that Christ had gone. And we saw the temple. In Christ's time it had been about the third temple built. The second one was built around 516 B.C. [Ezra and Nehemiah]. The third one was built by Herod. It was small compared to what Herod wanted, but it was sturdy and some of the stones were eighteen feet thick, some of them were as big as a house.

As Christ and his disciples were leaving the temple, they went up in the hills to spend a night and the disciples were saying that the temple would last until eternity. But Jesus replied, not a stone will be left standing. When they got to the Mount of Olives, the disciples asked Him what He meant. They were all sure about this time that His life was going to be over; they had a premonition about it. There was building hatred toward him.

Christ predicted the things that were going to take place. He told them that the temple was going to be destroyed, and that the other Jerusalem to be destroyed would be at the coming of the judgment.

Jesus discussed with His twelve disciples the terrible days coming ahead. He told them, "I'm going to be dead. I'm going to be gone and you must carry on my work." He told them they would suffer; they would be accused of being fakes, even devils, betrayers of God; they would be hated and killed and betrayed, even by some of the members of their own families. . . .

But Christ did not say, "Aha, when I'm gone you're going to have to suffer." He said, "You will suffer, but you'll have my protection and my love. I love you." And the disciples knew that whatever happened to them Christ would be with them every minute in the Holy Spirit. He loves us, too, and He told us, as well, that we all have the opportunity to be with Him every minute of our lives if we want to.

Jesus stands at the door and knocks [Revelation 3:20], but He can't break down the door. He doesn't want to. It must be opened by our understanding. It must be self-willed. And His work has to be carried on by those of us who love Christ. If we don't carry it on, it won't be carried on at all. We are the Johns and Peters and Matthews and Pauls.

Carter discussed the apocalyptic, which he said literally means the uncovering or the unveiling aspect of Matthew 24.

The return of Christ will be accompanied by cosmic changes—tidal waves and earthquakes. . . . He says there will be signs that knowledgeable people can't understand, but yet He didn't predict the date or the time. He talks about the fig tree, the most common tree found in Palestine. When the fig tree puts forth its leaves, summer is near. In like manner you can see the signs of Christ's coming.

Carter compared the second coming to the flood.

Only Noah [Genesis 6:13] knew that the world was going to be destroyed. His neighbors did not know anything. You can imagine what Noah went through living back in the mountains building his ship. You can imagine what the neighbors said to him. The ridicule must have been unbearable, but his faith let him survive.

Suppose you were informed this afternoon that Jesus was going to come tonight and you had just five more hours to live. What would we do to get ready for Christ's presence? You might think of all the people you had hurt, or of those for whom you had some hatred in your heart, and you might get on the phone and call them and say, "Look, I'm sorry." You might talk to your wife about something you had said to her, you might think of something you had never admitted you had done, or of something you hadn't been able to carry out or someone you had intended to witness to about Christ who had not known Him. And you might say to him, "Let me tell you about Christ dying on the cross."

But those things we would do in those final hours are the things we should be doing this afternoon. We should live our lives as though Christ were going to come this afternoon, so we would be prepared when Christ put out His hand and said, "Frank, or Clarence, or Hugh [Frank Williams, Clarence Dodson, and Hugh Carter, members of his Bible class], here we are together now." Jesus hasn't told us when He's coming, but we should be ready. And if there is something in our lives that we should change before Christ comes, let's do it.

Men's Bible Class, Plains Baptist Church, March 28, 1976

EQUAL IN THE EYES OF GOD

WE'VE SEEN IN THE ANCIENT CHURCH, and we'll try to bring it up to modern times, Christianity with life in it but also with conflict in it. Hard, tough debate, sometimes even animosities develop, and divisions within the church. [Many] new Baptist churches have been formed because of divisions among the old. When one part of the congregation split off, sometimes the new church would be bigger than the original church was. Then they could become friends again. The church I attended in Atlanta was an outgrowth of a division in the church. But back in the early days some divisions almost destroyed the church.

All early Christians who took part in the day of Pentecost, who had been visited by the Holy Spirit, who were bound together in a common commitment to Christ, were Jews, all of them. It was quite a while later before there was a willingness, even on the part of Jesus' disciples, to understand what Christ [meant] when he said, Go throughout the whole world and preach the gospel to man [Mark 16:15]. Paul, Peter, John, James, Matthew, Barnabas, Timothy—all of them—felt that the message of Christ was to the Jews only.

There evolved on the outskirts of the Christian church some [other] believers in Christ. One of these was a man named Cornelius, a powerful, strong Roman soldier who lived at Caesarea [Acts 10]. . . . Peter was staying about thirty-five miles down the coast with some friends at a place called Joppa. I've been through Caesarea. It came late; it doesn't show up on any early maps. It was there when Christ lived and when the disciples began to spread the gospel. Now it's just an ancient remnant of a city, nobody is living there. Caesarea came and left, probably because of the impact of the Roman army. Cornelius was filled with a love of Christ. He [wanted] to know how to go about being converted, saved, and baptized, to become a part of the church itself. So he prayed to God and received a message from God to send three people down to Joppa to find Peter. Peter was staying with a tanner named Simon. . . . Peter had a dream. He dreamed of a big sheet [covered] with animals, fish, and birds and reptiles. And God told Peter, "Take of this conglomeration of creatures and eat it." Peter said, "No, God, I won't eat anything unclean." And the second time, the voice of God came and said, "Eat it." And Peter said, "I won't eat anything unclean." And the third time the voice said, "Arise, Peter, slay and eat" [11:7]. This was in direct violation of the Jewish rules concerning food. Finally, God said, in an angry voice, "What God hath cleansed, call thou not that common. Anything I've cleansed don't call unclean" [11:9]. Peter did not know what the dream meant, and awoke at just that time three Gentiles representing Cornelius knocked on his door and asked Peter to come to Cornelius' house.

. . . . Now Jerusalem was still the head church among Christians; churches formed around the new Christian world were outgrowths of that church in Jerusalem. The concentration of authority and power, as it related to doctrine, was still in Jerusalem. The head of the church in Jerusalem was James, the half-brother of Jesus. He kind of controlled the church leaders who determined the doctrine of the church. Peter knew he was on shaky ground; he was not explaining his actions. This was a radical departure from what had been done in the past.

"Then hath God also to the Gentiles granted repentance unto life." This is a turning point in the church. If anything ever disturbed the existing church in the most intense way, it was this. Jews are proud people. For 2,000 years or more they had been told "You are the chosen people of God." When a few of the Jews accepted Christ as their Saviour, Christ being a Jew, they naturally felt *they* were then the true chosen people of God; the Messiah had come to them. They had never heard of the Messiah coming to witness to Greeks or Romans or non-Jews. It took the voice of God, the presence of the Holy Spirit, the voice of angels, to make Peter do it. He had never been in the house of a Gentile before. He walked into Cornelius' house, and asked him, "Have you been baptized?" He said, "I've been baptized. . . ." Peter said, "That's not the ultimate baptism. You've been baptized with water, you need to be baptized with the Holy Spirit." Peter testified also, later on in Jerusalem when the subject came up in the church synod, that . . . the Holy Spirit was there, just as it was on the day of Pentecost, . . . when the Holy Spirit descended on the original church members. Peter testified in the strongest possible way to these doubting leaders of the church that the Holy Spirit was there just like it was at Pentecost. Those who had doubted very much "when they heard these things they held their peace and glorified God, saying God hath also to the Gentiles granted repentance unto life" [11:18]. An internal church argument was resolved temporarily [but] it kept coming up again.

The Judaizers felt, despite what Peter had learned, that you couldn't be a Christian unless. . . . A Gentile could be a Christian, [but] he first had to go through the Jewish law, be circumcised, be like a Jew. . . . Everywhere there was a church this came up—in Galatia, in Asia Minor, Caesarea. . . .

Peter, as we all know, was a weak person. He was a big, brawny, muscular fisherman, impetuous—he was the one who jumped in the water and swam to the shore when he saw Christ after the Resurrection [John 21:27]. He was the one who dashed to the tomb when John held back [20:4]. But Peter was also the one who denied Christ three times. . . . After his experience with Cornelius, he, as a Jew, sat down with the Gentile Christians to eat; he talked with them at the supper table, something he never would have done before. [But when] he heard James was on the way to

Antioch with the church elders, Peter quit eating with the Gentile Christians; he separated himself off in a corner and began to insinuate that other Jewish Christians ought to keep themselves [Galatians 2:12–13]. . . . He weakened when the test came. He did not want to face the church elders, even though God had told him he was right.

Paul, a much stronger man, was willing to face the Judaizers. . . . He and Barnabas, who were missionaries from the Antioch church, were the most aggressive missionaries. They were constantly preaching among the Gentiles, . . . constantly witnessing to Gentiles and telling them they were equals. . . . A lot of the early members of the church, even after Cornelius' experience, said, "You have the love of Christ, but you also have to have the Jewish law to have salvation." That's not what Paul and Barnabas had been preaching. That was the test case that came up when Paul gave his letter to the Galatians, a test . . . for the entire world that knew Christ. Paul said the way to salvation was through Jesus Christ—period. You didn't have to be circumcised, you didn't have to study the Jewish law, you had to accept Christ. . . . If you believe in Christ, that's salvation. . . .

It shows the weakness of many Christians. When we're put under pressure in the world around us, even though we know the pure teachings of Christ, even though we know the perfect example of the life of Christ, we do just like Peter did. We yield, we back down, we apologize, we stay silent, under pressure. So we're not in a position to criticize Peter.

It shows also how strong and effective a Christian like Paul can be. Sometimes we even have to dispute and criticize other Christians. If we act through God, God said, "Judge not, that ye be not judged" [Matthew 7:1]. But he didn't mean a Christian should overlook false doctrines, that a Christian should overlook hatred, discrimination, injustice, insensitivity, an absence of love. God wants us, as Christians, to be strong and forceful leaders in implementing the teachings of His kingdom and following the pattern set for us by Christ. . . .

I would really hate to get in a debate with Paul. Quite an argument! He said that Peter was so influential that even Barnabas followed Peter in his withdrawal from the Gentiles. He asks Peter, "If you, being a Jew, live like the Gentiles do and not as a Jew, then why do you try to make the Gentiles live like the Jews? We who are Jews by nature"—he was kind of kidding Peter a little bit—"knowing that a man is not justified by the law but by the faith of Jesus Christ, even we have believed in Christ that we might be justified by the faith of Christ, and not by the works of the law, for by the works of the law shall no flesh be justified."

It couldn't possibly be said any clearer. Paul, by that time, had become the leading preacher, evangelist, of the church. . . . He was so forceful, so secure, such a powerful person, so logical in his explanations, that he was able to prevail.

Paul was a man who did not believe in a split-level church because Christ also had not believed in a split-level church. Sometimes even in our modern day we think there are different kinds of Christians—maybe white Christians are better than black Christians, Southern Christians are better than Northern Christians, Christians in a small, stable community are better than Christians in transient, larger, impersonal churches. That is not the way the church is. It's not the way Christ taught. . . . The fact that someone lucky enough to have been born a

Jew—Paul himself was a Jew—did not give them any exalted position in the church. That early test was resolved; it's been used for us to be taught for 2,000 years. But [the argument] still exists.

[When] we get involved in a debate or war with other people we've always assumed that God was on our side, that we were acting in accordance with God's will. . . . The first time that thought was ever shaken [as I understand] was in Vietnam and Cambodia, perhaps in Korea. Now there's a reassessment in our nation. Perhaps it's good for us, because, as with the early Jewish Christians, in the eyes of God we're no better than anyone else. We're not saved because we're Americans; we're not saved because we come from a community that's stable; we're not saved because our parents were Christians; we're saved because God loves us; we're saved by grace through one required attitude—that's faith in Christ. We're saved by grace through faith in Christ. So is everybody else. So is everybody else.

Men's Bible Class, Plains Baptist Church, June 20, 1976

THE SIMPLE FAITH OF LOVE WITH SIMPLE JUSTICE

The previous Thursday Jimmy Carter had won the Democratic presidential nomination. In his acceptance speech in Madison Square Garden, New York City, he had quoted Reinhold Niebuhr's words: "Love must be aggressively translated into simple justice." The next Sunday, he taught an overflow class in the up-

stairs assembly room at the Plains Baptist Church. The biblical text was the basis for his acceptance speech, I John 4, a chapter about love. The class began by reading in unison several verses, including 4:11: "Beloved, if God so loved us, we ought also to love one another.

One of the most profound challenges to the Christian church is to teach properly, accurately, and personally, and not to be persuaded with false doctrines. Most of you realize the Baptist church is almost unique. It was founded in this country, about the time Rhode Island was formed, in a deep search for complete autonomy in separation of religion from politics or church from state. Baptists always have been deep believers in the proposition that the believer is a saint—the sainthood of all believers—the belief that each person has a direct relationship with God. Each Baptist church is autonomous. We accept no domination from the Southern Baptist Convention or any other entity. In the church itself we believe very deeply that each person should have a direct relationship with God through Christ.

This morning we're going to be talking about this particular matter of false doctrines and false teachers. We'll be considering two parts of scripture—the last few verses of the Sermon on the Mount, Matthew 7:13 on, where Jesus talks about the falseness of a person's life. You can look at a person and he looks sound; you listen to him and he sounds as if he were stable and his life has a firm foundation. But Christ went on to point out that if you build a house on the sand, the first time the waves, the floods, the rains come, the house will fall. It might have been a well-constructed house, but because it did not have a foundation under it, it fell. If the same house is built on a rock, when the winds, the rains, the floods come, the house will stand.

It is the same way with a person's life. We might have the most brilliant intellect in the world, we might have studied under the great philosophers and theologians, we might have a Ph.D. or understanding of the interrelationship between people, but without a solid base under our lives, within our lives, all of that learning is superficial, and there's no foundation there for a meaningful existence.

In the early days in the church immediately following Christ's death, this struggle came to the forefront, expressed most vividly by the Apostle John. . . . John was a theologian. He tried to understand the interrelationship between the different struggling teachers in those early days. Christ's life had made a great impact throughout the regions surrounding the Mediterranean Sea. False doctrines and false prophets rose up. Christ himself predicted this.

One of the groups with whom John was struggling in the book of I John was Gnostics. These people were well educated; they professed to possess true knowledge. The word Gnostic means one who has knowledge, one who believes in knowledge. They almost worshiped knowledge. Gnostics departed radically from the basic tenets of the church as had been explained by Christ Himself and the apostles who learned at His feet.

In the Christian faith we believe that God came to earth as a human being in the person of Christ, that Christ was born of a virgin Mary. He lived and was tempted. He suffered physically; He lived the life of a person. In that process He became a man, at the same time retaining His identity as God. This is a teaching crucial to the Christian faith because it helps us understand what God is. John says no one has ever seen God. Jesus said, If you've seen Me, you've seen God [paraphrase of John 14:9]. We have a faith that's not elaborate; it's not mysterious; it's not designed just for college professors or those who have mastered the intricacies of language and logic. The Christian faith is very, very simple. When we reach a point in our lives—which probably occurs several times a day—when we want to know how to deal with an unforeseen circumstance or how to orient our lives toward a proper decision, when a difficulty presents itself to us, if we know Christ and if we ask ourselves a simple question, "What would Christ do?"—that gives us a simple answer to a very difficult circumstance.

So the struggle here in John's teachings is between the Gnostics, who worshiped knowledge and in that worship looked down on those who did not have much knowledge, and the Christian faith, which is filled with simplicity and purpose, simplicity of understanding. The Gnostics said, for instance, that the earth was created not by God. They felt that anything material was filthy and to be despised and inherently unworthy. They thought a lesser god had created the earth, that God himself didn't create the earth. They had believed that the serpent came not as a tempter, not as something wicked but to warn Adam and Eve about the wickedness of the earth. You can see they had gone into a very logical explanation of things. They also felt that after Christ was born and at the time He was baptized, at that moment the man Jesus who had not been God until that moment was filled with the Spirit and became Christ.

While Jesus was hanging on the cross, when He cried out, "My God, my God, why hast Thou forsaken Me?"

[165]

[Matthew 27:46], at that point the Spirit which was Christ left the man Jesus and went back to heaven. All these teachings could be proven to be cold analytical logic. But John said this contravenes the basic essence of Christianity. We have a need to understand the simplicity of the Christian faith [I John 4:1–6].

The first thing John says is to believe not every spirit. When John said try the spirits, he wasn't encouraging the sale of alcohol! To try the spirits means to test or put to the test the teachings that confront you. John goes on to say how to test the teachings of the spirit, whether they are of God. If they are of God, they teach the truth. If they are not of God but of the world, there is no way they can teach the truth. In Jesus' admonition at the end of the Sermon on the Mount, he had the same thought. He said, "Take two trees, there's no way a thistle can provide fruit, there's no way a bad tree can provide good fruit, there's no way a good tree can provide bad fruit" [paraphrase of Matthew 7:16–19].

A person becomes the kind of teachings that the person is. If a good person is founded on a proper faith, then the teaching of that person has to be good. John, toward the end of the first century, is teaching the same way in this letter probably written to the Ephesians, in what is now Asia Minor. Ephesus was a great city; it was one of conflicting doctrines and religions. John was very concerned about the Gnostics there. He said that it was important to remember that Jesus Christ is come in the flesh and that someone who teaches that is of God. The truth is that Christ came to be a human being, and those who teach that teach the message of God. He also points out that the coming of the anti-Christ has been predicted. Anti-Christ means against Christ or the personification of that which challenges or opposes Christ. John is the only one who ever uses that phrase—it's mentioned four times, in I, II, and III John. He says, "Ye are of God, little children, and have overcome the anti-Christ" [paraphrase of I John 4:4] which was already come into the world. He already has overcome the anti-Christ. He points out that it is the influence of the spirit we need to be concerned about. We need as Christians, as believers, to discern in our own minds what is truth and what is not truth. . . .

John of all the writers in the Bible personified the word "love." John is almost obsessed with the word "love." He starts off his admonition saying, "Beloved" [I John 4:1], and "beloved" means you who are loved by me. He calls the people of Ephesus, who are grown men and women, "little children" [I John 2:1]. He wasn't looking down on them, but he was their teacher, their instructor. He loved them as though they were his own children—John was very old at this time, maybe eighty-five to ninety.

John pointed out, too, that people have a tendency to be attracted by success, by a powerful popular exposition of a thought—the popularity of teachers attracts believers to them, even if it might be a false doctrine. We know John was telling the truth. But the test of the doctrine is over a long period of time. If you could ask people if they heard of Christianity, they would say yes, but if you asked them about Gnostics, most of them would say no. This is a kind of bandwagon effect, I guess. It's a part of the recognition of truth. . . . John says you'll hear all kinds of theologies—that's the studies of the different kinds of gods— but out of theology, which is very complicated, comes a simple message of love. God wants us to have an expression from Him through Christ of a simple message we can understand, even children four years old and people who have never been to school can understand.

What's the first verse you all learned? I learned one when I was four years old: "God is love" [I John 4:16], that this is a simple expression of faith: "God is love."

Out of love—and I put this in my acceptance speech the other night—has to come one more step: simple justice. You can't just encapsulate yourself in isolation or be a hermit and have love for people unless it's put into practice. Christ didn't get into an ivory tower and preach about love. John didn't go off by himself and hide in Jerusalem and preach about love. Paul was persecuted. He suffered in many ways in order to put into practical application the principles of the word "love." We have that responsibility in our own modern-day lives.

Too often the Christian church has formed a kind of mutual admiration society. We check off the folks who walk into church on Sunday and say, "Well, that person came to church, therefore that person might be almost as good as I am." You know that's not what Christ did. Christ was with sinners, despised prostitutes, cheaters, tax collectors, who habitually made their profit out of cheating people, common people, dark-skinned people. Remember the woman at the well [John 4]? The average person with whom Christ lived wouldn't speak to those who were of a different nature or different color or different religion, those [who were] lepers. Christ did. Do we do the same thing?

Quite often if you go into a Baptist church in an average town, certainly in the South, you find a social and economic elite. We're the ones who are kind of the prominent people in town. And we have a tendency, all of us—certainly I have myself—to think, because I have been accepted by God, because I have eternal life, because I have the peace of the presence of the Holy Spirit, because I have eternal salvation through Christ, I have a tendency to think I'm better than other people, that surely God must have recognized my worth and my goodness and therefore wanted me because I'm better than others. But we're saved through what? By grace.

Grace means a gift, a gift of God. Through what? Through faith. In whom? Christ. We're saved free by grace through faith in Christ. And when we have that faith, it is a humbling expression. We put ourselves, not above anybody, but below anybody. Christ more than anything else in his whole life on earth talked about pride, and deplored pride. Because He saw that when we think we're better than anyone else we almost are automatically separated from others. When his disciples struggled over who's going to sit at your right hand, who's going to sit at your left hand, who's going to be highest when we all go to heaven, Christ said the greatest among you are—what? Servants of all [Matthew 20:20–27]. I wish the Southern Baptist Church did what the Primitive Baptist Church does—the washing of feet—one of the most moving Christian experiences. Because you can imagine in a little tight-knit community like ours, there are always disharmonies. It's human nature. You get jealousies between people in business or competition. One farmer gets good rain, and makes a good profit. The farmer right next to him might have worked harder, misses the rain, and doesn't make as much of a profit. Tensions build up. And in the Primitive Baptist Church, I think once every quarter, or maybe every year, they have the foot-washing ceremony, because Christ said to do—by the way, they try to pick out the person from whom they feel most estranged and they get on their knees and wash the other person's feet. Christ did this.

One time when His disciples were arguing among themselves about who was the greatest, Christ got on his knees and said, "I'm just a servant" and He washed the disciple's feet.

Peter said, "No, don't do that." And Christ said, "If you love Me, you'll let Me do it" [paraphrase of John 13:5–17]. Love in isolation doesn't mean anything. But love, if applied to other people, can change their lives for the better through what I described to you as simple justice—fairness, equality, concern, compassion, redressing of grievances, elimination of inequalities, recognizing the poor are the ones who suffer the most even in our society, which is supposed to be fair. There's a great responsibility for those of us who believe in Christ. For us to sit in isolation and say blandly "I love everybody" means nothing. What is God? God is love. That's a very, very simple thing and it gives us unbounded opportunity to study, to learn, to challenge ourselves, to express our own lives in a meaningful way.

So if you're looking for something complicated, or wish to expand your tremendous mental capacity, that simple concept, "God is love," is a very challenging expression. Simplicity doesn't mean that there's not a challenge there. Christ points out that all of us sin. Christ says you're supposed to be perfect, but all of us sin and come short of the glory of God [Romans 3:23]. How to translate an understanding of Christ, the simple thing "God is love" into a meaningful Christian life, a closeness with God, a compatibility with what Christ did, is an unbelievably complicated and inspiring challenge for us all.

One of the favorite expressions I like to point out is by the theologian Paul Tillich, who said, religion is a search. It is a search for the truth about man's existence and man's relationship to God and man's relationship to other people. When we quit searching, we lose our religion; we become proud, self-satisfied, sure of ourselves. We anoint ourselves with a benediction and we lose that struggling to get back down where we ought to be in the spirit of a servant of others. The more powerful a person is, the less one has to prove his strength.

You've all seen I'm sure very small people physically, like a man who's five foot three. Quite often they'll be cocky, always having to prove that they're real men. But a great, strong, sure person need not prove it always. That's the way it is with Christ. And that's the way it is with Christians. When you're sure of your strength, you can exhibit compassion, emotion, love, concern, equality —and, even better than equality, the attitude of a servant. You can say, "I'm not only better than you, you're better than I am, and I want to work with you. So, theology, love, simple justice."

We ought to have a tendency in our own hearts and minds to search constantly for a way to make our own societal structure a better demonstration of what Christ is. That's what He told His disciples. We also are His disciples.

Here John expressed the essence of the Christian faith. In just a very few words, he said disregard all these false doctrines. This is what you need to know: Let us love one another [I John 4:7-12].

Dr. Martin Luther King, Sr., said the other night, "If you have any hatred left in your heart, get on your knees, get on your knees. It's a time to wipe away hatred and disharmony and animosities and distrust. Get on your knees and forgive those you feel hate you and vice versa. Jesus said, 'If you come to the altar with a gift and you've got hatred in your heart for anybody, set your gift over to the side, go find that person, be reconciled through love, then come back to the altar and worship God' " [paraphrase of Matthew 5:23–24].

That's what John is teaching here. "Let us love one another for love is of God. And everyone that loveth is born of God and knows God." He that loveth not can't know God" [I John 4:7]. So God is love. If you don't love other people there's no way to love God. "In this was manifested the love of God toward us"—for here's how God showed He loved us—because God sent His only be-gotten son into the world that we might live through Him [paraphrase of I John 4:9]. The only way we can have a meaningful life, the only way we can live, now or through eternity, is through Christ: "Herein is love, not that we loved God, but that He loved us" [I John 4:10]. We are not blessed with eternal life through Christ because we love God, but simply because "God loved us and sent His Son to be the propitiation for our sins" [paraphrase of I John 4:10].

We Christians know that, first of all, "All have sinned, and come short of the glory of God" [Romans 3:23]. "The wages of sin is death" [Romans 6:23]. God can't look on sinfulness and say, "That's okay." God's perfect, God's holy. He can't say, "All you sinful people, what you do is okay with me. Go ahead and sin, I love you anyway." God loves us, but He cannot say that sin is all right. All who sin—Sunday-school teachers, preachers, priests, bishops, people who never come to church—in God's eyes, we're all sinners. I don't believe God says, "Here's one person who is more sinful than another." I don't think He ranks us in an order. He loves us all. "All have sinned, and come short of the glory of God" [Romans 3:23]. "The wages of sin"—what does God owe us? Death [Romans 6:23]. But God loves us so much that He sent His only Son to take the punishment for our sin.

One of the most difficult verses in the whole Bible is one where He cried out when He was on the cross: "My God, my God, why hast thou forsaken me?" [Matthew 27:46]. We know that as Christ approached the cross He went off by Himself in the Garden of Gethsemane and said, "God, please don't make me do this. Please take this cup from me. But if you want me to, Thy will be done" [paraphrase of Matthew 26:36–39]. As Christ hung on the cross, He suffered because it was just as though He had sinned. It was just as though He had done all the wicked things we've done.

When we've lied, when we've hated, when we've cheated, when we've committed adultery, when we've stolen, when we've grasped for money—it's just as though Christ Himself had done those things. Because He took on Him and in His heart our sins, and, being perfect, He suffered even more than we would have suffered, perhaps. A man who is loyal to his wife twenty years and then commits adultery in a weak moment would suffer much more after that act than someone who never did care for his wife and always has lived in a sinful way.

Christ is perfect. As He hung on the cross He was, in effect, a sinner. He took the punishment for our sins. If we recognize that fact, that Christ is the son of God, He took the punishment for our sins. If we have faith in Him, then what can we have? Eternal life. We can be reconciled to God. We can be forgiven for our sins.

It's just as though we had never sinned. God doesn't say, "I still remember that sin you committed a month ago."

If we say, "God, forgive me, I put my sins on Jesus Christ, I'll let Him take the punishment for my sins. I believe He is Your son. I ask You to let me be reconciled to You, brought back to You through Christ," if you do that, you'll have eternal life. And in that moment—it's so easy to do—Christ comes into our heart and we have a new life through Christ with God. It's not complicated, there's no trick to it, but it requires humility. "God, I know Jesus Christ is your son. Christ is God. He'll take my sins. He loves me, I love Him. I'll let Christ have my sins, white as snow, all my sins forgiven, I have eternal life." In that moment we take Christ in our hearts, we're brothers and sisters with one Father who is God.

That is the point that John is making. In that process we not only love God and He loves us, but at the moment we begin to demonstrate our love, not with a halo, not in isolation, not in pride, but by showing we love our fellow human beings the same way Christ loved them, the same way Christ loves us.

Jesus said, "Everybody that yells on the judgment day, 'Lord, Lord,' will not join me in my Kingdom" [paraphrase of Matthew 7:21]. Jesus said people that keep the word of God—"Thou shalt love thy neighbour as thyself" [Matthew 22:39]—that person will be reconciled with Christ in heaven. It's not complicated; it's very demanding; it's not easy. That's the essence of the lesson. We hear all kinds of teachings, read all kinds of newspaper stories, all kinds of evils, books, and explanations. But the teachings of God are simple and personal. They apply to us. You don't have to have a preacher, you don't even have to have a Sunday-school teacher. You have to have simple faith.

Men's Bible Class, Plains Baptist Church, July 18, 1976

ADMITTING SIN

Carter said it probably was the last time he would teach the Men's Bible Class in the Plains Baptist Church for a while. Soon he would leave for Washington to be inaugurated as president. The lesson on this day was, "Jesus faces His call," drawn from Mark 1:4–13, the story of Christ entering adulthood and preparing for his ministry.

Carter began by asking questions: "Why are we here? What can we accomplish in our life span of a few years in a world of two or three billion persons? How can we actually be important or significant?" He invited answers. Various men replied "by being born again" or "by following the life of Jesus."

Only can we be worthy if we can approach closeness to God. That's done through Jesus Christ. That's why God sent His only Son, Jesus Christ, to die on the cross. God took the punishment for our sins through Christ.

It's very difficult for proud people to admit we're sinful. . . . Because of the color of our skin, our material wealth, we Americans tend to think, [others] are not worth as much as one American. That's the kind of pride that separates us from God. It's hard for us to admit we're sinful. It's very hard to say "I'm sinful." . . .

Christians are taught that God will forgive us. The fact that we know we will be forgiven makes it easy for us to say, "I'm sinful; I put wealth above compassion and caring, I put myself above others." . . .

[175]

Jesus suffered so much . . . became dirty, sinful, in effect, because He became guilty of our sins—that is what reconciles us to God because a perfect Jesus Christ became sinful like we are. . . .

I feel in my own life that Jesus is aware of my sinfulness when I am proud, or aloof, or self-centered. . . . I have a tendency to conceal it, not only from God but from myself.

During a witnessing mission several years ago, another person and I went to a woman's home. I'll never forget it. We started talking about the plan of salvation . . . a congenial discussion. When I quoted Romans 3:23, "For all have sinned, and come short of the glory of God," she got absolutely furious. "I'm not sinful; I'm a good woman!" She made us leave her house. There was no way for her to admit. . . .

The No. 1 issue is pride. . . . We have the same inclination in the Baptist church. People in the United States are guilty of pride.

Christ is our redeemer. Christ is with us. Christ said, "If you've seen me, you've seen the Father" [paraphrase of John 14:9]. In spite of our sinfulness, God loves us. We can have eternal life. Jesus came to show He was human but God also. Being both proves to us who believe in Him we can be reconciled to God.

Men's Bible Class, Plains Baptist Church, January 9, 1977

THE KINGDOM OF GOD AND THE CHURCH

The lesson was on the relationship between Jesus and Caiaphas, the high priest, one of four persons affected by Jesus that the class was studying. The others were Judas Iscariot, the Apostle Peter, and Pontius Pilate. The texts were Matthew 26:3–5 and 63–68, Mark 14:61–65 and John 2:13–16. Carter said Caiaphas' relationship was the most difficult.

The Roman government gave the high priest tremendous authority over the Jews. For eighteen years Caiaphas was "President, Congress and the Supreme Court." Caiaphas told the Pharisees, "You do not realize it is to your interest that one man should die for the people, instead of the whole nation being destroyed" [paraphrase of John 11:50].

Jesus challenged Caiaphas' authority by driving moneychangers and sellers of oxen, sheep, and doves out of the temple. The profits from the sales had been Caiaphas' source of wealth. Then Jesus healed the man with a withered hand on the Sabbath in contravention of temple law. That was a turning point in Jesus' life. He had directly challenged, in a fatal way, the existing church. And there was no possible way for the Jewish leaders to avoid the challenge. So they decided to kill Jesus.

Caiaphas represents an attitude that is part of all of us. There is a danger of the church of Christ becoming anti-Christ because, if we start to worship ourselves, there is a great temptation for us to set up our own standards. There is a danger that we may become proud and consider ourselves exceptions in God's eyes. . . . Complacency and pride separate us from God.

Why did God inspire Matthew, Mark, and John to write about Caiaphas? To let us see in ourselves the defects of Caiaphas, to strip them away and recommit ourselves to Christ. God has blessed us so much that we need to ask ourselves how we can help establish the Kingdom of God on earth.

Carter said he had conferred in the Oval Office with Spencer W. Kimball, president of the Church of Jesus Christ of Latter-Day Saints. Kimball had just returned from South America where twenty-six thousand Mormon young men are giving two years of their lives in missionary work.

"Why don't we call for the Baptist church to send ten thousand to twenty thousand young men and women . . . overseas?" I asked.

I think it might be good for us to think how the Kingdom of God, through our church, can be expanded in the years to come. Jesus' last words were to go through all the world to tell the world about Him [Mark 16:15]. I would like every one of us to feel challenged by a recognition of our own shortcomings and to serve as Christ did. We have a great blessing and a great love for God that we can precipitate even more than the message by Caiaphas through John and Mark and Matthew. Don't be like Caiaphas.

Christ rose from the dead on the third day and lives today in heaven and in our hearts. How alive is He in our hearts? No matter how dedicated we are, the limits of Christ can be for us so much higher than we can realize in our actions, our attitudes, our love.

Couples' Class, First Baptist Church, Washington, D.C., March 20, 1977

THE DOCTRINE OF FAITH AND SALVATION

It was the Sunday after what Carter had described as his presidency's most important week, when he had presented his energy plan to the nation. The lesson topic was entitled, "True to the Gospel," drawn from I Timothy 1:3–20. Carter started by talking of the Baptists.

Baptists always have been a little bit careful about the work "doctrine." We call ourselves a creedless church. The hierarchal arrangement in the Baptist church is very difficult to detect and certainly impossible to define. We believe in the priesthood of believers. Each Baptist looks on the church not as a mechanism to control our lives in toto . . . but a way to come together to exchange our personal, individualistic ideas about Christ and our relationship with Him. We have a deep pride in that sense of independence. When our country was in the formative stage, Roger Williams of Rhode Island was concerned that nine colonies had already established official churches; there was a great aversion in the hearts and minds of Baptists to a relationship between the church and state that was official. Historically, Baptists always have been cautious about creeds, doctrine . . . .

What is the significance of doctrine then? *Members of the class said it was "very important" or "stimulates debate."* It's like a skeleton in the human body. What was the main thrust of Paul's pastoral letters to the Corinthians, Galatians, and Thessalonians? "Feed the church," "Don't let them fall into error."

What method did Paul use to keep the young churches from falling into error? He tried to lay down and explain Christian doctrine. This gives us a paradox in our own lives: we have an aversion to other people telling us how to worship; at the same time, we recognize that Paul saw some of the dangers of the young, struggling, embryonic church. False doctrine was . . . a danger to the very existence of Christianity. . . .

What is the main thrust of I Timothy 1? Paul tells Timothy to observe correct doctrine.

Paul is concerned as he goes to Macedonia. He tells Timothy, "I heard you were staying in Ephesus to make sure certain men don't teach strange and false doctrine." So doctrine is important; we don't have the authority from God to try our own doctrine. . . . [we don't have] freedom to adopt a doctrine suitable to our own lives. That is not what the priesthood of believers means. It does not mean we're each free from any constraints. We are all subject to a rigid set of guidelines in our lives. Written by the president of the Baptist World Federation? Southern Baptist Convention? No. By the pastor? No. . . . Derived from what source? The Bible.

There's something unique about Christianity. . . . Christ is the center of our lives. A life of sharing. Caring, sensitivity, compassion, forgiveness, remembering the Lord's Prayer, abundant life, full life; a constantly growing, eternal life, love, service, spiritual laws. *The class has mentioned a number of these and Carter repeats them.* How many of those do you find in other religions? Love? Yes. Growth, compassion, truthfulness, honesty, unselfishness. So what's different about Christianity? Immortality? Christianity is not the only religion that believes in immortality. . . . There is something absolutely unique about Christianity: We believe in a personal relationship to a living God in Christ.

Someone whispers, "That's it."

Other religions don't have that. There's not a personal relationship between the worshiper and . . . God. This is a very important difference.

. . . Christ . . . . Son of God and Son of Man.

The Teaching Mission

. . . How close do you feel to Jesus as deity? When you think about god, the sun god, the stone god, there's a distance there; many people have a vast, unapproachable god. [But] Christ, the Son of God, referred to himself most frequently as Son of Man. Here again is a paradox. We think about God as remote, perfect, worshipful, unapproachable. We also think about God as close. "Father," that's part of it, but also as "brother." Christ was our brother because we have the same father. There's a closeness, a personal relationship we have with our father.

Jesus told the disciples he was the Son of God. In many ways he proved it. But if you had seen Jesus as Peter saw him, and someone said "describe him," you might have said poor, dirty, dusty. What kind of house did he have? He didn't have one. How did he relate to authorities? He was kind of a wanted criminal. Radical? Yes. It's hard to believe someone like that could be God. Did he ever get hungry? Yes. Was he ever tempted? Yes. Worshiped by everybody who saw him? No. Despised, hated? Yes. When he spoke a few words of truth was it inevitable that everyone would believe him? No. . . .

So here's a dual relationship we have, recognizing the humanity of Christ, making us feel that we are part of God's kingdom.

When do we have eternal life? Right now! We're coming to the front end of eternal life now. We've already begun our eternal life. We don't have to wait until we're dead to have it. We have eternal life now. We have begun a life with God. Where do we get our eternal life from? God. Why? Because Christ died for us; he loved us.

What about the merit of it? Is there a distinction in God's eyes between different levels of worship? Maybe some of you have children who are different from one

[181]

another. It may be one is practically perfect; maybe the other one you have a lot of trouble with. Which one do you love the more? A lot of times the one you have the trouble with. Even in our fallible, human minds, we don't say, "If you're perfect, I love you; if you're imperfect, I hate you." That's like God.

Of all the great leaders and teachers in the Bible, who are the ones we think about, who are central to our lives? Peter? John? Paul? Who was the greatest teacher? I'd say Paul. What are some of the characteristics of Paul? Dynamic, scholarly, learned. How about courage? Did he back down? Absolutely not. Temperamental? He didn't let people push him around. . . . When you think about what a Christian ought to be—those things describe Paul.

Paul in this letter to Timothy says, "Go out in Ephesus with all your strength and your ability and stamp out false doctrine." He didn't want to embarrass Timothy by saying, "This is the doctrine I want to teach you." So Paul describes to Timothy, in kind of an off-hand way, Christian doctrine. What do you see as the essence of Christian doctrine? Stewardship—giving of your life. Love and charity. First of all, Paul is talking about dedicating our own life to God. . . . We've got to have something first—faith.

I Timothy 1:5 is read.

This describes in a succinct way some of the elements of Christian doctrine: "charity out of a pure heart, a good conscience, and faith unfeigned." Paul is telling Timothy: These are some of the elements of a testament of the doctrine you should espouse. As you eliminate the preoccupation of the early Christian leaders who were sidetracked by idle conversation, debate, and genealogy, the idea that because of your own status in life you have a special position from God. That's not true.

What is faith? One definition is union with the living Christ. Sometimes it's hard for us to maintain. It's not easy in all the minutes of the day for us to have closeness or union with Christ. What does union mean? Be *one;* be one with the living Christ. I have one measuring stick of faith to show the degree of faith, how closely we measure up to that definition—union with the living Christ. It's a difficult thing to do, because sometimes we withdraw from Christ. We go about our daily business, grasping for money, pushing people out of the way, telling little white lies, not being quite kind enough to the person we're with. Then, if we're growing Christians, we are conscious of our limitations. We stop a minute and say, "Where am I? What am I doing? I've lost something that stabilizes my life." If we are in our office, or walking through a park, we might pause a minute, bow our hearts and say, "God, forgive me," and we draw back to Christ. Paul told Timothy, "You can't stand up to false doctrines unless you have an awareness of charity and faith . . . being close to the living Christ."

We've described Paul as someone very terrific. Let's see how accurate we are. If somebody asks me to describe myself, I say I'm fifty-two, from Georgia, a naval officer, president of the United States, a politician, a farmer, with a wife and four children, a Christian, a religious man. Did Paul describe himself the same way we do? Blasphemer, persecutor, "the worst sinner of them all." Does this shake our respect and admiration for Paul? He said, "I'm the worst sinner of them all." He admitted it and asked for forgiveness. . . .

How many of us can say, "I'm the worst sinner of them

all"? "We go to Sunday school on Sundays—a lot of people don't. We believe in Christ—a lot of people don't.
We've not committed murder or adultery—a lot of people
do. We don't destroy our body with alcohol and drugs—a
lot of people do. So how can we say that we're "the worst
sinners of all"?

Paul sees within his own black heart the wickedness,
sinfulness, lies, persecution, blasphemy, the temptations
to which he succumbed. Paul is courageous to identify his
own sins. He can't accurately identify other people's sins;
neither can you nor I. One of the greatest potentially false
doctrines and teachings of Christ is for us to violate what
Christ said, "Judge not, that ye be not judged. When
you're upset with the speck in your brother's eye, you
ought to be worried about the beam in your own eye . . ."
[Matthew 7:1–3]. The superficial, man-made doctrine. If
you go to Sunday school on Sunday morning, if you go to
the First Baptist Church, if you believe in Christ, that
makes you somehow better than other people. I'm sure the
sinner's admiration in the early church for Paul was, "He
set a standard for us." Paul said, "I know; I know. I can
look within my own heart. I'm the worst sinner of them
all."

God forgives, "He let me see; even though I'm imperfect, he let me be a witness."

Paul's point about doctrine is: God doesn't save us because we're good or better than anyone else. God saves us
because he loves us and Christ died for our sins. In order
to be forgiven for your sins you have to repent. What pre-
cedes repentance? An acknowledgment of our sins.

Suppose we kneel down at our bed at night and say,
"Lord, forgive me of all my sins. . . ." I don't believe it
works unless we're willing to say:

"God, today I was not kind to my husband or wife, my children."

"God, today in a business transaction I cheated a little bit."

"God, today most of the time I was separated from you."

"God, today I told two or three lies or misled people a bit."

"God, today I had a chance to do some kind things or I had a chance to forgive someone I had hatred for and who hurt me. I didn't."

Enumerate them! Call them by name. Under those circumstances all your sins are wiped away.

Paul didn't say, "I did bad." He *enumerated*. . . . Paul gave to Timothy a kind of personal testimony. What did God do for you? What did Christ's living and dying mean to you? Has your life been changed by Christ? Can you tell a stranger that Christ is God? How do you know? Can we say, like Paul, "I can tell you why." God loves us. That's what Paul tells us to do. Stewardship, yes. Was Paul just talking to Timothy? He was talking to Jimmy Carter and you.

What is the doctrine of the Christian faith? Jesus came forth as the Son of God. For what purpose? To save sinners. Faith is union with the living Christ. The reason Christ came to earth was to save sinners. Like them? Like us. That's why the Baptists don't have a creed. We have a faith . . . the living God, the living Christ, loves us. It's simple. God is love, personal and demanding. Did Paul tell Timothy to sit on your cushion at home, a good boy, and enjoy the blessing and knowledge of Christ, stay away from wicked people? No. That's false doctrine.

Paul, Mark, Peter—all completely willing to give their lives for Christ. Their lives already had been given to

Christ. They already had begun eternal life. Sometimes we think we're good enough, we'll be rewarded. We aren't good enough—but through Christ. . . .

The church—First Baptist Church, Southern Baptist Convention, Christian churches of all kinds—the purpose of the church is to preserve and teach a sound doctrine, based on the unique part of the Christian faith, a living Christ, God and our brother—distant, to be revered and feared; close, to be loved, to set a pattern for our lives, to shape our lives. Sound doctrine is the gospel of saving grace.

The major thrust of this morning's lesson . . . is to equate the knowledge of the doctrine . . . absolutely, with the way we live. Because if we didn't know that Christ was God, God is love . . . if we have all this in our hearts, it's not very meaningful unless it affects the way we live and teach and reach out, the way we affect people's lives. Christ said, "Go ye into all the world and preach the Gospel" [Mark 16:15]. Paul said to Timothy, "Go out, as I did in my fumbling way, and preach the doctrine." The doctrine has got to be equated with our own life experience to be meaningful. This experience is rooted in realization, not guilt. It is not a sad message Paul gave Timothy . . . it's not a sorrowful message but one filled with joy—happy, anticipating pleasure, satisfaction. Paul knew he was sinful but he is forgiven, and eternal life is starting now. . . . So what are we waiting for? Are we waiting for retirement? Are we waiting for more economic security? Are we waiting to realize our utmost human ambition? For wealth, prestige, prominence? Are we waiting for our children to leave home so we can have time to devote to serving Christ? What are we waiting for? Eternal life has already begun. Are we living now the way we'd like? Or for something better to come along?

. . . Christianity should be dynamic, searching, striving. . . . We drift—"Someday when it's not so embarrassing I'm really going to tell people what Christ means to me. . . ."

God's kingdom is not remote, on top of a white cloud. Christ said God's kingdom can be around the Christian. There's a little bit, a piece of God's kingdom, and we're in the middle of it. "Thy Kingdom come." There's only one way God's kingdom can come on earth, and that's through us. We're kind of proud; we're the epitome of the evangelistic, the well-organized, rich, affluent. We must spread God's kingdom by the influence of your life and my life. Or do you hope other Christians will do the things you or I don't do?

Paul points out that, in spite of our weakness, in our lives we have constant union with the living Christ. Put ourselves in a compatible relationship with Timothy and let Paul talk to us.

Couples' Class, First Baptist Church, Washington, D.C., April 24, 1977

NO GRAVEN IMAGE

How MANY OF YOU KNOW which commandment is most often mentioned throughout the Old Testament?

Several persons mentioned the commandments on killing, adultery, and loving God.

You're all wrong! I'll give you a hint. . . . This commandment of all the other commandments is the most frequently discussed in the Old Testament. It is the one that preoccupied Moses and the Prophets. Deuteronomy 4 in its entirety is a discourse on this particular commandment. . . .

"Thou shalt not make unto me any graven image, or any likeness of anything that is in heaven above, or that is in the earth beneath, or that is in the water under the earth: Thou shalt not bow down thyself to them, nor serve them: for I the Lord thy God am a jealous God, visiting upon the children unto the third and fourth generation of them that hate me" [paraphrase of Exodus 20:4–5].

It's a powerful admonition. I don't know of any of the other commandments where God puts such an intense admonition or threat to those who violate it. God goes on to say, if a parent violates this commandment, what will happen? The third and fourth generations will suffer because of this. It might be good for us to consider this commandment. We don't very often. . . .

Do we have graven images in our own churches? . . . What is the symbol we see most frequently in our churches? The cross. We don't worship the cross as such and I don't believe God deplores that we have crosses in our church because it's a reminder of what we believe, a statement to separate Christians from those apart from God . . . an indication that Christ is important to us.

In a lot of homes in poverty-stricken areas, in our own country, in Latin American countries, quite often there will be a painting of Christ, surrounded by colorful flowers or shining light bulbs. This doesn't mean we are substituting the painting for God.

So what does God mean by this commandment? . . . What kind of graven image? . . . Obviously we shouldn't have a graven image of a false god, like a cow or a beautiful woman like Diana [the virgin goddess of fertility (Acts 19:34)] . . . or anyone who has preeminence over God or [is] a substitute for God, [or something] we substitute for God, like social prestige, wealth, beautiful homes, worshiping it instead of Him. . . .

Symbolism, though, is very important. . . . The Ark of the Covenant was not a substitute for God. . . . Other symbols—wells . . . lavish stone walls, ladders dreamed about—have had a significant meaning for those people. I've been to Bethel with Rosalynn where Jacob dreamed about ladders [Genesis 28:12] and I thought about the yearning of people to have private contact with God. . . .

"How can I approach God? . . . He might condemn me. He might not forgive my sins. Maybe I can make an image or picture of God, or maybe I can have a stone with a cross at its head, as a substitute for God, because I'm not worthy to communicate directly with God." So the yearning of a human being to communicate with God has always been a difficult thing. Man has tried these symbols as a substitute for that interconnection. . . . We consider God to be unapproachable. What is God that He should be unapproachable? Where is God? Is He ensconced on top of a mountain, hiding in a bush, sitting on a cloud in heaven?

Where is God? In the midst of His people. In what form? Spirit, yes! "God is a Spirit: and they that worship Him must worship Him in spirit and in truth" [John 4:24]. . . . Spirit is an intangible thing. Spirit is also an illusion. A spirit is also a sense of feeling among human beings. What kind of spirit do you have? Happiness, despair, hope, longing, frustration, fear—the spirit of a person. "God is a spirit. . . . [We] worship Him in spirit and in truth." Truth is also an intangible. What does truth look like? How much does it weigh? Where is it? It doesn't mean truth doesn't exist because you can't weigh it.

Mercy, justice, love. What is God? Jesus said, "God is love" [I John 4:16]. Is love the kind of thing you can feel? Is love something that is close and intimate within your heart and within your mind? To the extent we try to establish graven images even of our own God in a very juvenile, very infantile way, we try to find what God is—a little golden toy—we destroy the essence of God and we substitute something that we design for omniscience, omnipotence, omnipresence, Creator of the universe, who knows our every thought, who knows every hair on our head, where every sparrow falls. We try to mold a crummy, despicable image to substitute for God.

Turning away from God to worship a graven image will hurt not only you but the influences you have on your children and then on their children, to make them suffer for your own sins. God is not mean and vicious and filled with hatred. But God said, if you hate me, then it will have a deleterious effect on you and on the people you will love. Of all the Ten Commandments this is the one most often overlooked. The strange thing, though, it is the one most emphasized in the Bible. . . .

Our own definition of God, our own definition of what's good, is based on what we are. . . .

[Jeremiah stood in the gate of the temple and said those who worship Jehovah in the temple lie because they worship Baal outside (Jeremiah 7:8–10).] No one condemns this beautiful building. We look on it as a house of God. We also have a strong inclination to substitute it for God, for spirit, for love. Many of us feel we fulfill our obligation to God by coming here on Sunday morning to Sunday school. . . . We go back home and feel holy because a lot of people in our country don't go to church or Sunday school. . . . Better than two-thirds of the people don't. . . . It gives us a certain social prestige; it doesn't hurt us in our business; it doesn't hurt in politics. How do you think God feels about that sense of pride and self-justification in His house? . . . We tend to substitute religion for our daily living habits. "He's a religious man, she's a religious woman, working for foreign missions." The word religion means to us some degree of achievement, justifiable self-pride. To the extent we let sin and self have approbation we become like the Pharisee, "I thank God I'm not like other men" [paraphrase of Luke 18:10–11] . . . It is a natural instinct. . . . Because that is *the* thing that separates you from me. That is what creates a quandary within us.

There is an image of God? There is an image of God. A perfect image of God. Christ. Can we envision what God is? . . . We can envision Christ because He is one of us. He was a Spirit and He was close to us. We have through Christ the perfect image of God that God told us to worship. . . .

I have a tendency to think God will be much more kind to me in church or in a far-distant place. But when I think about Christ, I think about Jesus walking down a dusty road, being spat upon, helping people find love, being gentle . . . I think about Jesus concerned about the crippled, or despised, or rich and despised. This is exactly what thing God is. That distance that separates us has now been removed. . . . A theologian named Martin Buber said faith is holy insecurity.* We ought not to feel

---

* See Maurice S. Friedman, *Martin Buber: The Life of Dialogue* (Chicago: University of Chicago Press, 1955), p. 114; and Paul Arthur Schilpp and Maurice Friedman, eds., *The Philosophy of Martin Buber* (La Salle, Ill.: Open Court, 1967), p. 232.

self-reliant purely within ourselves. When we proceed without God, without Christ, our lives are not complete. . . . We search for a substitute for God because our faith is not complete, because we feel a little bit insecure. . . . Because our faith is not complete in God the Spirit, in Jesus who is God, we tend to take out extra insurance by a church or some other graven image. . . . Because we do have a lack of faith we tend to create images for God. It's much easier to conform our own lives to the standards in this church, even, as measured by the other members than the perfection of us demanded by Christ: "I won't compare myself to what Christ wanted, I compare myself to my neighbor. It's a lot easier. . . ."

The church tends to reaffirm our self-esteem. We think a lot of ourselves. . . . The church tends to avoid making harsh criticism, the condemnation of sin. In the church where I grew up, the subject of the sermon was quite often "by God's word, you're going to hell. Because of your sin, you deserve death." We don't have that kind of sermon. . . . The church is not as condemnatory toward us as God is. . . .

We tend too much to trust in ourselves, [in our] material achievement in society. . . . "I stood on my own two feet and my achievements are mine." It's a kind of symbol of masculinity to be self-reliant. "I don't need your hand, God, I don't need You. . . . Because of my own worth, my own ability, my own strength, I'm pretty well able to trust in myself." Quite often self-worship is just as much a substitute, even worse, than a church building.

Jesus tells us . . . to open ourselves to God through the Bible as we read His word. . . . The difficult thing is to turn to Him and forget about the graven image—through Christ, though Christ Himself is a . . . stumbling block to the Jews. We know Christ is God, we know Christ is love, we know Christ is in our own hearts, minds, consciousness, around us and with us, if we will be receptive and tear down the human-created barriers we've constructed against us as a substitute for God Himself.

A class member asked about civil government.

I think there is a danger in making civil government an image—the word "jingoism" is a description of that. We tend to substitute a nation or a flag or a way of life or a government for God. It gives us a sense of superiority, which we don't deserve.

A woman asked if Americans put their trust in government and not in God.

I think the answer is yes. I had a long talk with Arthur F. Burns, then chairman of the Federal Reserve Board. We talked about the abandonment of Christian values in this country—hard work, family, clean streets, plenty of flowers, cleaning up the neighborhood, respect for authority and law, the value of human compassion. If we doubled our national budget we couldn't restore those values. . . . The perfect example of Christ is what our nation ought to be.

Couples' Class, First Baptist Church, Washington, D.C.,
July 31, 1977

BREAKING DOWN THE BARRIERS

The subject was the story of Jesus' conversation with the woman at the well. It was a remarkable meeting. Jesus had been called the Son of God; she was a lonely woman who had lived with six men. He was a Jew; she was a Samaritan, despised by the Jews. He was a man and she was a woman.

In 1976 I was at the Southern Baptist Convention. There were seventeen thousand or eighteen thousand people there. I was present as a Southern Baptist leader, as a member of the Brotherhood Commission, and as an ex-governor. . . . Three of us were there to represent the men of the church. When I looked at the program I was first very concerned and then immediately afterward relieved. The first speaker in that first session was Billy Graham. I was speaking immediately after him. Then I saw the person speaking after me was a truck driver. I was told he was not illiterate but not a well-educated man, very rough hewn. Billy Graham gave one of his usual very forceful, very important talks. I talked for about five minutes. The truck driver had never made a speech in his life. He was completely drenched with sweat, and as I sat there with him on the speakers' platform, he said to me, "I don't think I can get through it." Then he got up and said he had been a drunkard and he had found Christ. He didn't know what to do about it. He didn't have many friends. He was pretty well isolated from the rest of the world because of the life he had lived except for people like him who hung around bars in the small town where he lived.

He wanted to witness to Christ, so he decided to go back into the bars. At first he was the subject of scorn and animosity. The bartender said, "You're ruining our business here." He kept on going to bars and he would talk to anybody who would listen about his changed life in Christ. Eventually they looked forward to seeing him come into the bar. People gathered around and asked him questions. "I wasn't learned in the Bible. I had to get scripture from my new Christian friends around church," he said. "They kept asking me questions I couldn't answer. I went and got the answers and came back." Fourteen or fifteen of his friends came to Christ.

Well, you can imagine what the highlight of the whole convention was. It wasn't my speech as a well-known candidate for President, as an ex-governor. It wasn't Billy Graham. It was the truck driver. I don't think anybody who went to the convention will ever forget that frightened, bumbling statement.

I don't know who the "outstanding" Sunday-school teacher or college professor or insurance executive or business leader was who had talked to that drunken truck driver. . . . I don't think that person, months after his personal expression to the truck driver of what Christ meant to him, a fine, upright, clean, decent, probably wealthy businessman, I don't think he could foresee that truck driver would be speaking to eighteen thousand Baptist leaders. Somebody bridged the chasm between us fine Christian people and him.

The same thing happened in the fourth chapter of John. That truck driver became centered around Christ. He studied, he worked, preparing himself to go among his old friends. Most of us live the life of Christ, and attend Sunday school and church. We come once a week to church regularly. We live a full life during the week, preparing ourselves intently for the sale of insurance or, in my case, making decisions that affect the foreign policy of our country, or carrying out our daily professional lives. The dedication of our lives is the thing we put paramount. . . .

Part of the struggle that separates institutional religion,

you might say instant religion, from the ministry or the gospel of Christ, the natural instinct of any religion on earth, including our own, is to feel superior to ourselves, to have a sense of belonging, the alleviation of fear, a binding of a common group with whom we feel at ease. The gospel of Christ stands in vivid contrast to that. We are the insecure that Christ sought. Even his disciples often fell far short of his example.

The lesson this morning touches on that daily conflict. We ought to think about where we stand. Have we created chasms around ourselves that separate us from those who need and hunger for the gospel of Christ? Is our primary goal in life as Christians to husband to ourselves the mercy of God, the forgiveness of our sins, the knowledge of Christ that gives us truth? Or is it to tear down barriers, to reach out and share, to affect other people's lives in a benevolent way and an unselfish way, and, at the same time, to expand our own lives, instead of being narrow. . . ?

Carter told of seeing Man of La Mancha, *a play in which Don Quixote meets Aldonza, a prostitute. She slaps him away in scorn. But he transformed her life.*

The Man of La Mancha exalted her from her absolute sinfulness and her life was changed. This has happened in my own life on several occasions. When I was a deacon in the church in Plains, I went out and witnessed to people who were looked upon as alienated. I've seen their lives transformed, not because of me but because of a new awakening in their hearts that they meant something to God. It meant something to me. Tearing down of barriers is one of the responsibilities of a Christian.

If you look at a map you'll note that Samaria separated

Judea from Galilee. It lay on the western side of the Jordan River. Ordinarily, when Jews had to go from Galilee down to Jerusalem, they crossed the Jordan River and went down the East Bank and then crossed back to go to Jerusalem to keep from going through Samaria. Quite a bit out of the way. But when Jesus and his disciples traveled . . . they decided to go through Samaria.

There was an extreme division between Jews and the Samaritans, probably because of historical animosities. For eight or ten centuries the kingdom of the Jews was divided between the northern and southern kingdoms. After the Jews were captured by the Assyrians and taken into captivity, the Assyrians moved into the area around Samaria. The Jews and others who came back from captivity looked upon the Samaritans as barbarians. When the Jews finally came back into Jerusalem and began to rebuild the temple, the Samaritans came to help build the temple. The Jews said, No stay away, we don't want to have our temple defiled.

So it was a shock to the disciples when Jesus went through Samaria. There Jesus met the Samaritan woman at the well. . . . It was strictly forbidden for any religious Jew to speak to a strange woman. A sex chasm or discrimination . . . was quite strictly observed. Also, the Samaritans were dark-skinned people looked down upon as racial outcasts. They were not considered worthy, not even considered as being in the category of human beings by some of the more fervent racists among the Jews.

. . . The well was Jacob's well, a well-known well. Nobody was there when He arrived except this woman. What do you think the normal pattern of life would be to and from this well? People lived in nearby towns, say a couple of miles away at Sychar. . . . Every evening when it got cool and the fieldwork was done, the women would walk together to the well in a spirit of friendship, talking about the day's events. It became a social thing to go to the well for water. It was a mandatory act in the life of those people.

There was a significance in this woman's being by herself, as Jesus saw. She was an outcast. If somebody had asked in Sychar who the most sinful person was, chances might be they'd say this woman is the most sinful of us all. Here was Christ, perfectly secure, without sin, comforting a woman who was the epitome of sin. It was a vivid contrast. Did Jesus know about this woman's character when he spoke to her? What did he ask her for first? For a drink of water. Did she have another cup or dipper with her? No. So what was He going to do? He was going to drink of her cup, where her lips had been, where her hands had been. He was going to drink out of the same vessel she used. . . .

She couldn't believe it. "Why are you talking to me, why are you speaking to me? You're a Jew, I'm a Samaritan. You're a man, I'm a woman" [paraphrase of John 4:9]. So the encounter was a bridging of a tremendous chasm or gap.

When Jesus' disciples returned from Sychar, they were quite surprised. Perhaps their opinion of Jesus fell some, that he would associate himself with this kind of woman.

What was the woman's reaction to Christ? . . . She was embarrassed. She didn't quite know how to handle it. What was Jesus' point in the encounter He pursued? To get a drink of water.

She had often deceived; she didn't want Jesus to know about her. She knew Jesus knew she was a Samaritan and a woman but she had a lot more behind her. And Jesus, contemplative, said, "Where's your husband?" What did she say? "I don't have a husband." Jesus then said, "That's right, because the man you're living with now is not your husband and you've lived with five other men before this" [paraphrase of John 4:16–18]. Did she run away? No, she didn't. I think the natural thing for a woman like that to do would be to cover her face with a veil and take her bucket and leave because it must have been excruciatingly embarrassing for her.

Why do you think she stayed? She was astounded to know He knew. That certainly intrigued her, someone like a fortune teller told her life. A feeling of hope. Fear, yes. . . . She probably asked herself what is this power this man has? There was something else. "Are you a prophet?" She wanted to know more about him. . . . I think the reason she didn't run away at first was that she . . . was a lonely woman. None of the other women, who were self-respecting, would speak to her. I doubt if she had anybody to talk to except the men who wanted her. She had been a despised person and perhaps had a lack of self-respect and worth. . . .

Here was someone who transformed her instantly. The fact that He said, "You've had five men" was significant . . . because He had spoken to her knowing that. . . . I'm sure the thought went through her mind, "This man asked me for a drink of water out of my bucket and he drank of my water, and he knew who I was." She realized instantly, "There is at least one person on earth who thinks I'm somebody, who thinks I can be at least a transient friend."

Then Jesus speaks to her of something he could provide that was even more significant, "living water," welling up like a spring. She said, in effect, "Nobody can do that."

Except the Messiah. And Jesus said, "The man you're talking to is the Messiah" [paraphrase of John 4:26]. I'm not a good historian of the Bible, but I'm not sure He had told His fellow Jews that. . . . He hadn't told His own disciples; He certainly hadn't told the priests in the synagogue. . . . He had not stood on the street corner, and said, "I am Christ, the Son of God, I am the Messiah."

Why do you think He told her? Why do you think He singled her out . . . ? She was more open. She brought up the subject. She asked Him. She needed Him. She really needed Him. If anybody ever needed Him, she did. She moved from . . . alienation and consternation to casual conversation, to a realization of friendship so deep they drank out of the same bucket, to saying, "Are you a fortune teller or prophet?" to a realization that in spite of her sins He cared for her, to a belief He might be as great as Jacob, to a hope He might be the Son of God.

I wouldn't have known had I not studied the lesson this morning that there was a difference in how the Samaritans and the Jews looked upon the Messiah. What was the difference? What kind of a Messiah were the Jews looking for? A king, somebody like David, who would come in and lead them and cast away the Romans and set himself up as a religious and temporal ruler. That's what the Jews wanted; that's what Jesus did not want.

But the Samaritans? What were they looking for in a Messiah? A person who could tell you all things. . . . Is that a David? It wasn't a ruler but a teacher, a religious teacher to explain the mysteries of life that concern people—about sin, redemption, salvation, how to bridge the gap not between two people but between me and God. That is what the Samaritans were looking for—not David but Moses. They wanted to be delivered, to be taught;

they wanted to be brought back to God. They wanted to be saved, spiritually. Jesus recognized in this woman a representative of the Samaritans who wanted the kind of Messiah that He was, not a Messiah that would strike down the Roman soldier, who rode on a black horse. So He said, "The one you are waiting for, the Messiah, is the man you are talking to" [paraphrase of John 4:26].

The disciples came back and she went into the town. . . . She was joyous. Does the Bible say that she was excited? She forgot her bucket, of all things! . . . I guess one of the precious things she had was her bucket, and she ran off and left it. . . . She had already recognized and demonstrated by her act that the teachings of Christ were true.

She gave Him a drink of water; He had given her eternal, living water. She ran into the village, knowing about her reputation. She didn't run in and say, "I have met the Messiah!" She said, "I met a man who knew about my life." She said, in effect, "Is it possible this man might be the Messiah?" [paraphrase of John 4:29]. If she had gone in and said, "I have met the Messiah" . . . she might very well have been rejected. The way she expressed it created a mystery. . . . "Can this prophet be the Messiah?" She created an attitude among the people who lived in Sychar to let them take the initiative, to let those big shots in Sychar say, "Let us go and find out if this is the Messiah." She created in their minds an inquisitive attitude. . . . She used very good psychology. They came up and met Christ, and what was the result? Many of them believed.

Jesus stayed in Sychar a couple of days, not as a healer, not as a preacher, not as a teacher, but as the Son of God, as the Messiah. . . . They talked with Him and listened to Him. Many believed He was the Son of God.

So that was a special demonstration of repairing the divisions between us and our neighbor, us and the despised, and human beings and God. But the disciples were filled with consternation. I'm sure many of them knew He was the Son of God. But they were saying, "This is a precious bit of information we have. We know the Son of God. Someday in the future we're really going to tell people about it."

Jesus said: "This is the harvest. Why do you want to wait four months. Here it is right now, in this woman. This is the harvest, this despised Samaritan with a problem. You don't have to wait until we get to the Sea of Galilee. Here it is, right here!" [paraphrase of John 4:35].

The person you work with every day. The student who sits at the next desk. Members of your own families. Here it is, right here! What are you waiting for?

We break down the barriers sometimes in a highly publicized way. We've made a lot of progress in our country between black and white people. There's a tendency on our part to say, "You know, the Civil Rights Act and Martin Luther King, Jr.'s life work have solved that problem once and for all." Right? No. It's a continuing thing.

We have a tendency to rest on our laurels, to say, "Look at that, we weren't so bad, Congress passed a law. So we don't have to worry about that any more." We've broken down religious barriers. We permit, under our Constitution, Catholics, Jews, Moslems, and even atheists to live without persecution. So I as an American citizen and as a Christian don't have to worry about religious barriers any more because they're taken care of.

We don't have as easy a time with barriers of good vs. bad, pure vs. defiled. I'm sure when I say that, that almost all of you say, "He means that I'm good and he's witness-ing to the defiled and sinful." Sometimes the church creates a barrier itself because we tend to encapsulate our-selves in respectability, security, goodness, decency, re-ligious commitment. Amos said, "I hate and I despise your feasts and your institutions" [paraphrase of Amos 5:21]. He was talking about the church of his day. He said, "Let justice roll down like waters, and righteousness like an ever-flowing stream" [5:24, Revised Standard Ver-sion].

It was hard back in those days for justice and righteous-ness to roll down like waters out of the church, and it's hard today. Where is the water, where is the ever-flow-ing stream that can roll down out of the church, filled with righteousness and mercy? Where is that water? Our-selves. We are the rivers of water. We are the ever-flowing stream.

Is it dammed by our feeling that since we are secure, since we are part of God's community, since Christ does love us, since we read the Bible, that we can become still and at peace, and avoid suffering and exploitation? Most of us have an attitude that we've got it made, therefore we must be blessed with success. Why should we soil our-selves by coming in contact with those who are different, whose lives are filled with drunkenness, prostitution, or alienation, or crime, or sinfulness—"they're different."

. . . Christ and this woman had something in common. Christ looked back on this woman's life and saw sorrow, grief, suffering. Christ looked forward in his own life and saw sorrow, grief, alienation, suffering. They were tied together with not only a common hope but also a common human experience. Christ knew as vividly as though it al-ready had occurred about his future filled with despair.

That's why Christ reached out to Mary Magdalene and others who were despised. He didn't do it from up here, reaching down. He said, in effect, "I'm one of you."

Sometimes the hardest thing for a Baptist deacon or Sunday-school teacher or preacher to do is to say, "Im one of you." Not, "I'm better than you; I feel sorry for you; I'm here to give you part of my own business or my favored position with God; I'm here to share with you my superiority." It's almost impossible not to have that attitude, knowing that God loves us. But it should put me in a position of equality, of understanding, of comprehensive love, of compassion, of love with those who don't know Christ.

You can't witness to somebody from an ivory tower because people know our superficialities. We are not better in God's eyes than the prostitute in the world. We're sinful in the eyes of God. We're not saved because we're good. We're not better because we come to church. In the eyes of God all of us are sinful. We ought to serve God worthily just because we are church members. It takes a lot of courage, it takes a lot of comprehensive development. We can't do it by ourselves. The closer we live with Christ the more possible it is to reach out and let our own lives speak of the love of Christ.

When that woman came close to Christ she reached out: "Look what I've got. Look what I've found. My life has been changed. I'm here to tell you about it" [paraphrase of John 4:29]. The Samaritan woman had the same experience we can have—she learned Christ. She had an experience we ought to emulate, if we are as good as she. She had to tell somebody and she exemplified in her own action what Christ was and what she saw in Him.

So this is a good lesson. . . . This is what I want to

leave with you. . . . Somebody else doesn't build barriers around us. We are the ones who build barriers—to protect ourselves. We are the ones who have to tear down the barriers. We can get on our knees and pray:

"God show me how to tear down the barriers that separate me from you and others. Let me tear down the barriers that separate other people from you."

And I think God will do that.

> Couples' Class, First Baptist Church, Washington, D.C.,
> November 6, 1977

LIFE IN DEATH

The pre-Christmas Sunday-school lesson was about death, as Carter noted in the lesson, a curious juxtaposition with the celebration of the birth of Christ. The text was John 11, the story of Jesus raising Lazarus from the dead.

What is the essence of Christmas? What word describes it? Joy, love, peace, light. . . . A new life in Jesus. Death is in juxtaposition to life. It's hard for us to talk about Christmas when we think about death. . . .

I doubt if there is anyone here who hasn't experienced in our own families the excruciating experience of death, of someone we love. My father died fairly young of cancer. We know that many of the small children of our beloved friends lose their lives because of polio or some contagious disease or an accident.

We as devout Christians say, why did God do this? Why did God take away the life of this beautiful child?

Why did God take away the life of my father? There is a
concern about this in the Bible verses. One I memorized
in my Christian witness career, "For all have sinned, and
come short of the glory of God" [Romans 3:23], and another verse, "The wages of sin is death" [Romans 6:23].
We tend to have a feeling that God punishes us, because
we're sinful, by death. . . . So death becomes a horrible
punishment inflicted on us . . . terrible, heartbreaking
tragedy.

We think about people who are very seriously ill. We've
had the experience ourselves about someone saying, "She's
just given up hope." That's almost a death penalty. She
has ceased to struggle for life. Life has no more meaning,
and the prospect of death becomes almost inevitable. So
again, you have a strange conflict between clinging to life
and yielding to death, mutually incompatible.

Jesus, in this lesson, was describing someone who
bridged that gap. The reason for accepting physical death
as observed and described by Christ is profound, and important to us as Christians. We tend to make death in a
physical way very, very important. It is involved with
one's self. My own physical life is so important, my life is
important to me. We tend to think that our physical existence on earth is almost transcendent in significance to our
souls, even though in a moment of quiet or lucidity we
remember what the Bible teaches. It's almost impossible
for human beings to accept the fact that our own life span,
our days on earth, are not one of the most momentous and
important characteristics of existence.

This lesson is difficult to teach, but it's exciting to read.
We learn about Jesus' power over death, demonstrated in a
vivid, very dramatic way. I don't know of any story in the
Bible that is more exciting—maybe the Prodigal Son

[Luke 15] thrills you more or some other episode in Christ's life. But to me this is one of the most exciting stories in the whole Bible.

A number of years ago I was up in Connecticut on a Christian witnessing effort as part of our church's work. We were going from one home to another among people who couldn't speak English. They could only speak Spanish. I was traveling with a man, Eloy Cruz, a Cuban Baptist who now has a small church in Brooklyn. Eloy Cruz was going with me to a family who had no real knowledge of Christ, where there was nothing but poverty and despair and alienation and withdrawal from society. He would describe to them his own relationship with Christ, how much he loved them, how much Christ loved them. He would sit around in these sparsely furnished apartments and witness. Because of him, we felt the Holy Spirit was with us. We visited about one hundred homes during the week and all I contributed was—because of my halting Spanish—I could read from the Bible.

But in this particular case, we went to a home—I'll never forget—it had about four or five chairs around a small, cheap breakfast table. Eight or ten children looked out the door when we were coming. The man had a bottle of beer in his hand. . . . Eloy Cruz picked the eleventh chapter of John to read. . . . Jesus was threatened with the death of one of his friends. He went to visit his friend and found Lazarus was already dead. When Eloy Cruz read that Lazarus had come forth from the tomb, the children broke into cheers, applauded, shouted, screamed, and jumped up and down. I've never seen anything so dramatic.

But that's the way this story is. The knowledge that Christ has dominion over death also affects us. It's one of the crucial elements of Christian belief, that life does not terminate at the time of this physical death, that Christ has power or authority, demonstrably, in earthly terms, to prove that is true. It's something hard to believe on a scientifically analyzed basis. But the story of Lazarus, the story of Jesus, Mary, and Martha, is one of great hope to us.

When Jesus got the word, He was in Jerusalem and He was under attack. He had gone through most of his ministry. He had aroused the antagonism, hatred, fear, and envy of the religious leaders of that day, and, in effect, He was in hiding. That may be one reason why the word got to him late. Actually, Lazarus had been dead two days when word came that he was sick.

Jesus didn't want to be found. He was fearful; his disciples were fearful of their lives. He didn't want to leave hiding to go into Bethany to reveal himself. His disciples said, "Don't go." . . . Bethany is only a couple of miles outside of Jerusalem. It was not very far away. . . .

Martha believed Christ was the Son of God. She believed He had the power to prevent death. When she heard He was coming, she rushed out to meet Him and said, "If you only had been here, my brother would still be alive . . .

Jesus said, "Your brother will rise again." In His earlier discussion with the disciples, Jesus had said, this is an event that will exalt the Kingdom of God and will demonstrate the power of God. So His first remark to Martha was, "Don't be worried, your brother will rise from the dead."

Martha knew already the teachings of Christ. She apparently had been part of a relatively small but rapidly growing group who understood the theology that Christ had brought, that after death there would be life, a time of the last days when the dead would rise.

"Lord, I know that. I understand what you already said. I believe your teachings. You don't have to tell me. I'm thankful for the prospect of reunion with my brother in the last judgment day." She thought he meant the resurrection.

Christ made one of those profound statements that have shaken the history of the world: "I am the resurrection, and the life: he that believeth in me, though he were dead, yet shall he live" [11:25]. This is the essence of Christ's explanation of the significance of death. Through Christ, those who die will live.

I'm sure Christ knew of Martha's complete belief in Him. Here she says in an unequivocal way, "I know that anyone who believes in you will have life. I also know, friend Jesus, that you are the Son of God." There couldn't be a fairer expression of faith. It's the same faith we share. Our faith as Christians, almost two thousand years later, should be just as profound, just as sure, just as certain, just as intimate as that of Martha's. There's no reason why we, in the seclusion of our own homes, in the daily life we live, in a moment of quietness, can't say, "Jesus, my friend, I know that, through you, those that believe you have and will have everlasting life, and know that you're the Son of God."

We tend to exalt someone like Martha. But for millions of people, their faith, your faith, is equivalent to Martha's. It's a simple faith, it's not complicated. "Jesus, I know you are the Son of God. Jesus, I know that through you physical death has no meaning. After death, we can have life."

Jesus had walked out where the Jews, the friends of Martha and Mary, were lamenting Lazarus' death four days after the burial. In those days it was the common practice to have the burial the same day as death. . . . Jesus walked to the place where Lazarus was buried. . . . When He got there, He said a remarkable thing: "Roll the stone away." Martha thought immediately that He brought down the heavens, brought forward the resurrection day to that dusty place at Bethany where a stinking body was in a cave.

His friends said, "Lord, we can't do that because Lazarus stinks. He has been dead four days." And Jesus replied, "All of you are going to see the glory of God, if you believe."

I think at that point Martha had no inkling what was going to happen. Probably, she knew the possibility that Christ could reverse the death. She had said, "We know that you can overcome death, that through you there is eternal life." She said, "Lord, I know that if you had been here while he was alive, you could have kept him from dying." But even Martha, in her profound belief, never dreamed that a physical body that was already decomposing could be brought back to life.

Jesus said, "You're going to really see the glory of God."

. . . Christ knew His own life might be endangered further. In this group of mourners there were not only the immediate friends and perhaps relatives of Martha and Mary and Lazarus in Bethany. As in our own funeral services, the religious leaders were there also to join in sorrow. They weren't bad people; they cared about the problem of facing death. I'm sure they gave the proper prayers on the occasion of the passing of someone they loved. It was an orthodox funeral ceremony.

No doubt there must have been a shock when Lazarus came walking forth from the tomb where he had been dead four days, still wrapped in funeral clothes that bound him.

Jesus had already become suspect. He had shaken the foundation of the church and He had claimed to be, sometimes in definite words and actions, the Son of God. But there almost always had been a way to interpret His miracles so they could be discounted: it was an accident or trick, for someone who had been sick to have gotten well, for the lame to walk, that this guy who had been on the corner claiming to be blind wasn't really blind, but a beggar who claimed to be blind in order to get money without working. There had always been some rationalization. Religious leaders had said Jesus was not really the Son of God. It's impossible. A very tricky imposter, a very intelligent imposter, a magician, perhaps, or someone who could even hypnotize his audience, convincing them that things happened when they really didn't. And they had spared his life up until this moment. That final break with the characteristics of a human being had now occurred. Jesus could be compared to those around, compared to John the Baptist, compared to Moses, perhaps. So they had spared His life. To kill Him would have dramatized His importance; He would have been a martyr.

So they said, "Let the guy live, play it down. Ignore Him if you can. Discount His miracles. Dispute His claims. Say that He is not the Messiah, our Saviour, Christ, the Son of God." They just never thought Christ had power over the dominion of death.

This vivid demonstration of Christ's power brought about His death as quickly as could be arranged by the powerful religious leaders and Jesus knew it ahead of time. His disciples had the premonition. They, in effect, gave up the prospect that Christ might live.

And Lazarus lived. I presume Lazarus was still alive when Jesus died. We don't know how long Lazarus lived. How important was it that Lazarus live five more years? Everybody that lived then is dead. So the essence of the story, that Lazarus lived five more years isn't very important. What difference is it if we live fifty-six years or fifty-eight years or seventy-three years or eighty-four years?

Sometimes we have such an intense fear of death that we can't really live. The meaning of life is not in the number of years on earth. Everybody here, except one or two, is older than Christ was when he died. Martin Luther King, Jr., died a young man. John Kennedy died a young man. The average age of those who wrote the Declaration of Independence was about forty years young. Christ's ministry only lasted three years.

We tend to think that to exist for seventy, seventy-five years is a great achievement and very important. But Christ here is trying to show that victory over death can give meaning in our life. We should not be preoccupied with physical death; we should not be preoccupied with physical health. We should not be preoccupied with fame and reputation and social status.

The important thing was, "Lord, I believe in you. I can have eternal life. Those who believe in You can have eternal life."

When does eternal life begin for us? At death? Are we partaking now of part of our eternal life? Yes. We have too much tendency to say, "Someday, later on, I'm going to really start living the eternal life that Christ gave. I'm going to be a meaningful person. I'm going to do the things I've always known were right. I'm going to prepare for my life with Christ—someday. But for the time being, I'm going to cling to things given me—security, status, competence, happiness, gratification. But later, I'm going to join Christ in as perfect and intimate a fashion as possible."

Part of the lesson is, let's not wait until the day of our death to start to join the presence of Christ. A lot of people say this, "After death, I'll be with Christ. After death, the Holy Spirit will be part of my existence. After death, I'll know the meaning of God."

Christ says, forget about death and enjoy and appreciate and understand the meaning of life. We have seen, in this case, the sorrow of Martha and Mary and Lazarus' friends transformed into happiness and joy and exaltation and surprise and celebration, but we don't have to wait until we die, or to come back to life, or a miracle occurs, or we read about a miracle, to know joy, exaltation, fullness of life, celebration. Because God has already given it to us. To the extent that our life isn't full, [but is] filled with fear or trepidation or doubt or insecurity we're wasting it. We worry about ourselves in our human existence. It's really kind of a symbol of selfishness to concern ourselves about the limit of our physical existence.

I don't see any incompatibility between this story of death and the birth of Christ, because in the hearts and minds of those who learned that day and still learn about the resurrection of Lazarus, life began. Paul said that all those who believe in Christ have eternal life. Life begins now. Our relationship with Christ is of greater significance to our life than the shortness of our life, the absence of our life.

Jesus left the family facing His own death. So do Lazarus, Martha and Mary and Fred Gregg [teacher of the

class]. And so the degree of intimacy, love, and appreciation experienced by Martha, Mary, and Lazarus, we also
should experience. Just as Christ gave His life to Lazarus,
He gave His life for us, and what Jesus gave—the peace
and security and purpose that comes to us personally
through Christ—is just as good as it was on that day for
. . . the strength of a human being to illustrate the character of God, His spirit and the fact that He moved the
judgment day's raising of the dead to the present day in
our own lives. On the day we know Christ our eternal life
begins, and the rosy future which we set down when we
are going to restructure our lives is now.

> Couples' Class, First Baptist Church, Washington, D.C.,
> December 18, 1977

THE CREATIVITY OF ANXIETY

PAUL TILLICH said that for a Christian just having to live
and face a certain death creates enough anxiety for a
human being, and that the church in its teachings about
Christ should not add anxiety to a person's consciousness.
We have enough anxiety as it is.

The message of Christ, the relationship you have in
Christ, should not be built on fear but deliberately in-
stilled in our hearts, of God or of Christ.

Niebuhr says that anxiety is the basis for all human
creativity.* That's a very far-reaching statement. Niebuhr
is trying to say that anxiety, a kind of a negative word,

* See Reinhold Niebuhr, *Nature and Destiny of Man: A Christian Interpretation*,
vol. 2 (New York: Scribner's, 1953), p. 58.

the basis for all human fears, is a constant searching for ourselves.

One aspect of anxiety is the absence of satisfaction for the way things are. Anybody have any thoughts? How about someone who struggles always to improve one's self, to pray, to learn, and then attains a worthy objective. You set a goal for yourself, you work hard and you achieve it . . . a high goal for yourself. What's the normal response? The normal reaction would be preparation for the next goal, not to sit back and say, "Well, I'm twenty-five years old, I've graduated from college. I've graduated summa cum laude. I've got a good job. Now I'll relax the rest of my life." That's the kind of person who's driven to take advantage of the opportunities to stretch one's mind, to stretch one's heart, ordinarily will not, at any point in life, stop. The urge, when you see how much you can stretch your mind or heart, and that you can achieve a goal, creates in your mind an inclination to look beyond to set another goal and to work. That setting of goals that are doubtful of achievement, creates an uncertainty, an anxiety, doubt. . . .

What is there within the Christian's life that creates an anxiety or a need to higher accomplishments or creativity? As we read about and study the life of Christ, we probe our own consciousness. We have frequent confrontations with God or encounters with God and the despairing aspect of it that we as Christians know is that as we measure ourselves against God, we'll fall short. One of the things that Christ talked about more than any other subject—I haven't analyzed it word for word—is self-satisfaction, pride. "I've accomplished what I ought to as a Christian," which implies perfection. "I'm perfect, I'm equal with God." That's the very thing Christ warns us about. And the most notable example is the Pharisee's prayer. "I thank you I'm not as other men." And Jesus said, "That guy's praying to whom?" To himself! Jesus said he wasn't even praying to God [paraphrase of Luke 18:10–14].

So the failure of us all to measure up to God's expectations or man's laws creates a predictable and beneficial anxiety, a concern that we are not measuring up in God's standards.

One of the easily explained definitions of anxiety is awareness of one's own sins, which is a prerequisite to the redemptive plan of God. If we don't see that we have sinned, there's no way that we can be submissive or ask forgiveness or turn away from sin and be redeemed. On one of the missionary missions I have made in my life we went to see a woman. As we sort of explained the plan of salvation—and the verse we thought of was, "All have sinned" [Romans 3:23]—and she said, "Not so, not me." That's where the witnessing broke down, because she would never acknowledge the fact that she had sinned.

So anxiety is not necessarily a bad word. It creates a tension within ourselves which is an inspiration, a challenge, and a basis for self-condemnation or self-acknowledgment of inadequacy or sin. We try to overcome those anxieties, but, in effect, we never change one for another; we *substitute* one for another. . . . But we ought to be anxious about our shortcomings. We ought to be anxious about our lack of love of God. We ought to be concerned about how much more we can know about the world or about people around us. That's just part of it that may be beneficial.

But some other concerns and worries that preoccupy us are not of concern to God. What is one of the major, all-pervasive worries of human beings? Money, success. What's the most sure of all? Death. Death. We're concerned about death. Our concern is the result of elevating in our own mind the importance of our own human life. If we think that our existence is the most important of all, then to lose it is one of our most important losses. And, of course, this was not at all important to the teachings of Christ.

The most important single deed of the New Testament was what? Eternal life, as proven by resurrection of Jesus. Paul has said that without the resurrection there would be no purpose in His teaching or witnessing of the disciples. But, still, no one. . . . We are concerned about death.

Last weekend we were at the funeral of my Uncle Alton A. Carter, my father's only brother. All of us were very sad. The repetitive sorrow in our own lives, the deaths of our parents, the death of a child, the death of our spouse, and it's a time of crushing despair and sorrow.

One of the characteristics of that loss is exemplified by one of the first experiences in the life of a little child. All of you who have children or grandchildren know that a frequent dream of a young child is demonstrated when the child wakes up screaming in the middle of the night and the parent goes to comfort the little baby. "I thought you were gone! I thought you had left me!" The mother says, "I'm right here. . . ." When we lose the loved one . . . the sense of abandonment or aloneness, there's an empty space in our lives.

In one of Christ's final messages to His disciples, who loved Him and cared about Him and couldn't understand the interrelationship between a human existence and the thrust of Christ's ministry in His life, He tries to explain it to them: "In a little while, I'm going to be gone. I won't return, but I'm going to return temporarily." He's trying to convince them and us that we need not ever be alone, that we're not ever abandoned, that God always loves us.

In the King James version, "If ye love me, keep my commandments" [John 14:15]; in the RSV, "If you love me, you will keep my commandments." There's a difference. They are not in conflict, although they have a different emphasis. But here, in the initiation of one of the final speeches or talks of Christ to us, He's trying to show what love it. One of the remarkable demonstrations of love is what? Obedience. To keep the commandments. We can talk, attend Sunday school, sing hymns, put on a pious attitude, and prove, thereby, that we . . . that we don't really love Christ, we love ourselves. We love the approbation that comes to us from Christians as we pretend to love Christ . . . so the keeping of Christ's commandments is a necessary proof of whether or not we love Him. Christian love obeys.

The demand of God and the grace of God. The demand of God is quite stringent. How can we be perfect? Christ said, "Be perfect, . . ." [Matthew 5:18]. Not being perfect is sin. The grace of God means that regardless of our sin we are forgiven. With Christ, with God, we can overcome temptation and we can reach great heights of achievement; we can experience a genuine meaning of love, we can overcome our innate human selfishness. By ourselves. No. With Christ. Yes.

God gave us a will. He didn't make us automatons. He didn't say, "This is Jimmy Carter, I'll make him do this and that. He doesn't have a will of his own and, therefore, he'll be perfect because I'm controlling him." I have the power, the authority, to reject God if I wish.

Love is not a quiescent thing. It's not something that

you just kind of poke around and absorb. Christ's life is a demonstration of love. . . . Christ is teaching us in His life, His example, that love is an active thing, a demonstrable thing. We can isolate ourselves, not do anything, not hurt anybody—that would not be an expression of love. Love is a difficult thing. It's a precious thing, and, like almost every other precious thing it has a lot of counterfeits . . . a lot of false kinds of love that we tend to substitute for the more difficult thing. The more difficult kind of love is to act in concert with God to improve the lives of others. We kind of form partnerships with Christ to improve the lives of others—that's a demonstration of love. In the process—with Christ—we can forget about ourselves. We can even forget about getting credit for that accomplishment. We don't have to pray in public; we don't have to drop our money in the collection plate with a great clatter so everybody sees us; we don't have to push the fact that we love our neighbors. Genuine love can overcome human temptation for self-recognition. It has to be with and through Christ. But the bad thing about it is that almost two thousand years ago Christ died and His disciples who loved Him, knowing that He was faced with death, were bereft of consolation. They felt they were going to be abandoned. Christ spoke to reassure them and reassure us [John 14:16–17].

One of the most mysterious statements Christ made, one we cherish and that is an assuaging concept for our own lives, [refers to the Holy Spirit]. The Greek word is *parakletos.* We have a modern word, "paraclete." "Para" means "at one's side as a help," as a "paramedic" is one who is at the side of a doctor to help him. "Kletos" means "to call." To call to one's side to help. Jesus said, "I'm going to ask God to call someone to be at your side to help—at Jimmy Carter's side, at Fred Gregg's [the regular class teacher] side, at Paul's side, at Peter's side. There's going to be someone at *your* side to help" [John 14:16–17].

What are some of the functions of the Holy Spirit? He's an adviser, he's a counselor, a comforter, an advocate for us to God, a convictor, teacher, ever-present. As with Christ himself.

Christ pointed out, "My time on earth is limited." What else is there about the Holy Spirit? He's ever-present. He's not only to be here forever but he can be everywhere. Christ was subject to death—at least, in a physical form. He's a counselor, someone said a teacher, quite remarkable isn't it, for us—the person of the Holy Trinity about whom we know least of all. He's an extension of God's redemptive presence on earth after Christ. . . . The Holy Spirit is a personal reality that lives in the disciples of Christ and lets the word of Christ continue and prevail through us. What did Judas not Iscariot ask Jesus? Judas asked the same question we would ask: "Why didn't Jesus just, in a constant binding demonstration of godliness, all-powerfulness, miraculous presence, convince all the nonbelievers?" I think Jesus. . . . What would you do that would be more miraculous than to call Lazarus to come forth from the tomb when he had been dead four days and have Lazarus walk out? Or heal the blind? Or give the most exalted teachings on earth? Or demonstrate, in miraculous terms almost, the unique character of a love that would be so all pervasive that purity of life would have to be demonstrated by human beings. Jesus in his ministry had performed this remarkable, shocking thing, and many had reached out to Jesus.

How many of you have seen the movie *Oh God?* How many of you were disappointed and repelled by it? I thought it was one of the best movies I've seen. When I read about it, I thought it was terrible. I was afraid it [would be] sacrilegious to have George Burns as God! I would advise you and all Christians, if you haven't seen it, to go. I don't agree with all the movie [but] I would imagine the rejection of George Burns in the movie was very similar to the rejection of Christ when He was on earth. I don't say that in a sacrilegious way. I imagine it was just as hard for people back then to believe in Christ as the absolute Son of God as it was for John Denver and others. If you ran a public-opinion poll in Israel during the time of Christ's life—"Do you believe in Jesus as the Son of God, the Messiah?"—you [would] probably [have found] fewer saying yes than the number of people who supported the Panama Canal treaties a year ago. This one overwhelming proof brought thousands of people to Christ. This is a very difficult thing.

John 14:18 is read.

Love means what? Obedience. Love, obey—that is one of the most difficult ways to demonstrate love through faith. Christ said, "Through the Holy Spirit for those who love me and keep my word," God will love them and their existence, and their influence down through the ages, through all believers, through Judas not Iscariot, through Peter, through John, through whom else? Through us! The charge Christ gave His own disciples applies directly to us. We can witness, we can't carry on by ourselves.

Though we're weak, we're resentful, we're doubtful, we're lonely, we're not influential, we're insecure by ourselves, we need not ever feel alone. If we are doubtful, filled with anxiety, we need never be fearful, because with Christ, with the Holy Spirit, we're given the strength adequate to meet the responsibilities put on us by God. That's a big responsibility. With the Holy Spirit, with Christ, with God, we are strong enough, forceful enough, competent enough, brave enough to meet the responsibilities of God. . . . With that presence of God, with that partnership, we ourselves can perform on our own initiative, we can be rewarded.

John 14:25–27 is read.

Jesus said, "The holy comforter is coming in my name, in the name of Jesus." The Holy Spirit is with us and . . . torn by Jesus . . . and by a sense of abandon. I can walk without. Jesus said strike all those things. "Peace I leave with you. You'll never see me again. Peace I leave with you. My peace I give unto you." There was a peace that existed all around the earth then, the Pax Romana. Under the Romans, the subjugated people had lost the spirit to rebel and their physical needs were pretty well met. . . . Was that the peace Jesus was talking about? No. "Not as the world giveth give I unto you. Let not your heart be troubled, neither let it be afraid."

This is a very difficult lesson to understand. It's a very consoling lesson. It also puts the responsibility on us. Jesus didn't spread balm all around to make us impervious to tragedy or disappointment. When He said "With the Holy Spirit in your heart, those kinds of things are almost inconsequential." As a matter of fact, because of these problems we can be closer to God, closer to the reality of life, closer to personal fulfillment, closer to real peace, closer to happiness.

A lot of people identify our present age as the age of anxiety. We measure what we have so that we can have more in a physical sense. It creates in us a sense of inadequacy . . . that I failed by human standards and human measure. We forget about the fact that God's standards for a Christian are quite different. In this lesson are spelled out five standards by which we can measure ourselves. It's the test of a Christian.

1. A Christian must demonstrate obedience to God's commandments.

2. The presence of the Holy Spirit. There's not a Christian here who sometimes has not felt in a tangible way, a fruitful way, perhaps even a miraculous way, the presence of the Holy Spirit. It takes hold of our heart. In time when trial and tribulations and testing of God's will comes down, you've got to have some help.

3. A growing understanding, with the accent on growing, which means that all throughout life there's got to be searching for a deeper relationship with Christ through the Holy Spirit, a deeper relationship with our fellow human beings. . . . If we ever reach that plateau: "I have measured up to God's requirements. My life is a success. I'm an adequate Christian," that's when we lose something precious. We need to dig more deeply and grow in the understanding of God.

4. Our life must be consistent with Christ's life. We read in the New Testament what Christ actually did, what His life was about. . . . The thrust of our lives, the philosophy under which we ought to be consistent with the life of Christ.

5. An inner peace. It's not something you can will, as such. You can't say, "Tomorrow, I'm going to have inner peace in my heart." It slips away from us. It's not something guaranteed to each of us. It comes in the first four points—if we subjugate our lives to God, if we open our

hearts to the Holy Spirit, if our life is consistent with the purposes or example of Christ . . . in our relationship with God and others, then we will have inner peace. . . .

This lesson shows us a sense of offering of grace on the one hand, a sense of tough demands on the other, what our life is and should be and can be. After Christ died, and was buried, and was resurrected and joined God in heaven, it wasn't the end of the Christian era when Christ left this earth because in us is the Holy Spirit. . . . Christ's word can be still heard through the Holy Spirit—yes, but also through us.

Couples' Class, First Baptist Church, Washington, D.C., January 29, 1978

The Preaching Mission

On *several occasions Jimmy Carter has preached on personal faith in Christ. Two especially significant talks were given on the same day, June 18, 1976, when, in the morning, he spoke to several thousand laymen of the Disciples of Christ, gathered at Purdue University, on "The Standards God Demands" and in the evening, in Atlanta to a large audience of black preachers of the African Methodist Episcopal Church on "Down to Where the Suffering Is." These were the first major speeches Carter made after the presidential primaries. The next two talks included here— "On the Need for National Humility" and "Servants of God"— were given in Washington at the National Prayer Breakfast, sponsored by the prayer breakfast fellowship, in January 1977 and January 1978. The last, "The Inward and Outward Journey," was delivered before the Southern Baptist Brotherhood Commission, in Atlanta in June 1978. A number of the themes that emerge here, such as the sin of pride, unchanging faith, and the need for justice, have been characteristic of Carter's comments on religion over recent years.*

THE STANDARDS GOD DEMANDS

[THERE IS A] KIND OF A HUNGER among the American people for something that doesn't change. . . .

I didn't come here to preach to you. I'm not a preacher. I didn't come here to tell you what's right and wrong.

. . . I have a tendency to judge other people; I think everyone does who gets a captive audience like this. I am a farmer and my father's family have been farmers in Georgia for two hundred and ten years or so. When I was about five years old during the Depression years I first learned how to judge people. . . . Every year during the harvest season from July until about September when peanuts are ripe, I would go out in the fields every morning with a little homemade wagon and pull up the peanuts out of the ground and haul back to the yard. We didn't have running water or electricity, but I pumped water and washed them seven or eight times to get the dirt out of the peanuts and then put them in salt water to soak. Very early the following morning we got up and boiled those peanuts—the delicacy of the South is boiled peanuts. I would put about half a pound in a bag and I had about twenty bags every day. [With] a wicker basket . . . I walked about two and a half miles down the railroad track to the nearest metropolitan area, which is Plains, Georgia. It had then about six hundred people in it; it now has six hundred and eighty-three people in it. It was my first experience with urban life. I had a chance as I moved down the streets of Plains to learn even at that early age who the good people were and who the bad people were. The good people were the ones who bought boiled peanuts from me and the bad ones didn't. I haven't come any further in my ability to judge other people, so I'm not here to judge, not here to preach.

In the last eighteen months I've had a special opportunity to learn about our country, to travel throughout our nation, to talk to people, to answer questions, to get to know the consciousness of Americans. One of the most vivid impressions that I've had is the diversity that exists in our country. We're kind of the melting pot of the world. In agriculture, in business, professions, manufacturing, transportation, education, we have brought together different viewpoints, different problems, different needs, different hopes, different dreams, different aspirations, different prejudices, different fears. Quite often we tend to think the differences that exist among us are a source of weakness. That need not be true. One of the great innate natural strengths in our country is our ability to take different kinds of people and form a strong nation. Every one of us in this room has difference in our own being.

I am a husband of about thirty years; I'm a father of four children; I am a farmer; I'm an engineer; I'm a scientist; I'm a Christian; I'm a politician; I'm a businessman, and a lot of things that comprise my life. Each of you has the same series of different responsibilities, experiences, training, background in your own lives as individuals. That doesn't make you weak, provided we can take the best parts of every aspect of our lives and put them together and let that be us.

There's no reason why we should be less honest on Monday morning in our business or profession than we were Sunday morning as we taught Sunday school. There's no reason why we should care less as a governor of a state or as a schoolteacher about people as individuals, who look to us for leadership and who depend on us for the quality of their lives, compared to what we feel as we open the door and go into our own homes and embrace our wives or my little girl. But we tend to let the differences grow. One of the major thrusts of our religion, of Christianity, is to [let] what we learned about Christ, about God, about ethics, about morality, about truthfulness, honesty, brotherhood, be part of our lives.

It's very hard for men to do that because we have a tendency to want to show strength and independence and an absence of emotion. We're very reluctant to let anyone see us shed a tear even in moments of crises. We tend to isolate ourselves from an overdemonstration of love for another person. Pride is a natural aspect of the modern American man's life—to show that we've succeeded. We're proud we have a good reputation in the community. Pride separates us from a very important aspect of Christian life, the searching that comes from humility. If you analyze the parables of Christ, perhaps more than any other subject, Christ was concerned about pride.

The two men who went into a church to worship: One was a very fine community leader, a religious leader. He said, "Lord, I thank you I'm not like these other people. I tithe, I try to obey your rules, and I thank you for the blessing you've given me in letting me be such a good man." The other went in and prostrated himself and would not even raise his eyes onto heaven. He said, "Lord, have mercy on me, a sinner." And Christ said, "Which one do you think went away justified?" [Luke

18:10–14]. Obviously the one who had an adequate degree of humility.

This is another opportunity we have as Christian men to learn in a continuing way to strip away the artificial covering that enwraps our consciousness and our being even from our own self-analysis and lets us see that we're sinners.

We live in an unstable world. When I grew up on the farm, and you grew up twenty-five, thirty, forty years ago, there was a much more solid sense of belonging. When something happened to me as a child that was traumatic, or challenging, or fearsome, or disappointing, my mother and my father were always here. So were my brother and sisters. When I went home I knew there was something that didn't change. We lived in the same house, in the same community where my ancestors lived. That stability has changed now. Twenty per cent of the American people move every year. The family structure is not nearly as close as it was.

This has carried over into a loss of belief in the things we thought never would change. I always thought my political leaders told the truth and our nation stood for what was right in the eyes of God. Maybe it was too much of a natural pride. In the past few years, we've seen, with the Vietnam War, the bombing of Cambodia, the Watergate tragedy, the CIA revelations, that the goodness of our nation and the rightness of our nation is not as sure any more as it was.

So what does exist on a permanent basis? Obviously, a search for truth, a search for justice, a search for brotherhood, a search for love—our religious convictions don't change. They're there. But they're not there in an intense enough way and sometimes they're not there for other people because they can't be observed in us. We have a country that is searching for a basic integrity. We're searching for sensitivity about other's needs. We're searching for competence, ability. Sometimes the search is not as fruitful as we would like.

This puts a tremendous responsibility on us in this auditorium who have been blessed by God. I doubt if anyone in this room is hungry. I doubt if anyone in this room feels their children will never get an education. I doubt that anyone in this room is deprived of an adequate opportunity for preventive health care. I doubt that any in this room have immediate members of our families who are in prison or who depend on welfare payments to buy clothing. So we're blessed in material ways. This puts on us responsibility not to withdraw from involvement in the realization that many in our nation suffer from those deprivations.

We're not blessed because we're good or because we're better than others. We're blessed through the grace of God. The biggest blessing we have in our lives is our belief in Christ which gives us, depending upon the surety of our faith, an unchanging core around which our lives can function. That is an enormous benefit to us and a tremendous blessing.

I, like most of you, accepted Christ as my Saviour as a child, eleven years old. I was baptized in the church where my father's family had been. When I went to the U.S. Naval Academy in Annapolis as an eighteen-year-old midshipman, I taught Sunday school for three years to the junior boys and girls of enlisted men and officers who were stationed at Annapolis. When I went on a ship, including the submarine, on special days I would hold religious services for other members of the crew. When I came home from the Navy in 1953, I volunteered to be a Sunday-school teacher. I later became superintendent of the department. I later became a deacon in the church. I later became chairman of the board of deacons. I later became head of the brotherhood of men's work in thirty-four churches. I was very proud of my status in the church.

Then I began to realize that the personal relationship between me and Christ was not very significant in my life. I was asked to go by my church on what we call Pioneer Mission Work. We would leave our business for a week or two. We would go to areas in the nation, maybe in our own state or other states . . . through telephone calls we [would] identify families [where] there are no church members at all. We would get laymen to go into those communities to visit those families. We generally would try to see about one hundred families per week. It was a very exciting thing and a very difficult thing to do.

When I was asked to do this the first time, I said, first of all "I don't have time. I've got to get my crop planted." The Brotherhood leader said, "When do you get through planting your crop?"

I said, "Well, I won't get my crop planted probably until the middle of May."

He said, "Well, we happen to have a group going to Pennsylvania about the first of June."

I couldn't think of another excuse right off. I said, "Well, I'm really not trained for it." I had forgotten about all the great things I had done in my church. I said, "What do I have to do?"

He said, "You have to be willing to give one week of your life to God with no strings attached."

I started to say "That's easy." Then I realized that probably up to that moment I had never given an hour to God in my life with absolutely no strings attached. So I prayed about it and decided to go.

My life began to change because . . . the personal witnessing to other people about Christ forced me to reexamine who I was and where I was. I was fairly well educated and I was fairly prosperous; I had a good solid family. I belonged to the biggest church in town. But as I went from one home to another along with other laymen I saw how much more significant their lives were than mine. They were not as well educated or as prosperous as I was, but they had something in their lives that I didn't have, and I learned. I began to reexamine who I was and where I was going. Nothing I had ever achieved up until that moment had such satisfaction for me, and when I failed, I became bitter and very discouraged. But I began to see the simplicity of religious faith.

On one of my trips I went to Massachusetts. I was asked to go and witness among the Spanish-speaking people, mostly Puerto Ricans who had come to our country and who were not assimilated in our society yet. The Brotherhood commission found out I could speak Spanish. . . . I had learned my Spanish in the Navy and it was a completely different vocabulary [from] what I used. But I went with a Cuban pastor named Eloy Cruz, chunky, short, broad-shouldered, brown-skinned, the finest Christian I have known personally. . . . I was his assistant.

We would go to these homes where they were poor, alienated, withdrawn, sometimes filled with animosity, and I listened to the simple message . . . Eloy Cruz took to them. First of all, that they were sinners—and so are we, equally so. Those poor people thought we were much better than they. Eloy Cruz in just a few simple words said we're all sinners in the eys of God. Secondly he said, in spite of our sins God loves us, He loves you, He loves us. Third, he said, that God sent His only Son, Jesus Christ, to take the punishment for our sins. And if you believe that then you can be forgiven for your sins and have eternal life.

As we witnessed during that week, forty-six people, I think, accepted Christ as their Saviour. They formed a new church; it's still there. I learned from that good man.

Eloy Cruz explained theology to them. They didn't know the meaning of the word and I didn't know much about it either. He said, "You only have to have two loves in your lives. One is a love for God. The other is a love for the person who happens to be in front of you at any particular moment." That's a very difficult thing to do. It's easy to love your next-door neighbor who drives by your house in a Chrysler or Cadillac every Sunday morning on the way to church. It's easy to love black ladies in distant Africa or Asia. But to transfer your love repeatedly during the day, every day, to the person who happens to be with you at any moment is a very great challenge to us all.

I have seen lives changed and in the process had my own changed, and I've developed, I think, a strong desire to reassess constantly who I am and what I believe and what I do.

Paul Tillich, a great theologian, said that religion is a search for the truth about man's existence and his relationship to God and his fellow man. If you diagram the sentence you see religion as a search. When we quit searching for a deeper commitment to Christ and when we quit searching for a brutal awareness of our own sins and failures and when we quit searching for a deeper relationship to our fellow human beings, at that point, we lose a substantial part of our religion. Taking our status in life as an indication of God's approval of what we are and a recognition of our achievements and our worth as compared to others is a profound mistake.

What tremendous strength exists in this auditorium—four thousand or five thousand men, knowing the truth that never changes, having a pattern in the life of Christ that we have studied since we were children, having influence in the community, individually, through our families, through an organized church. What a tremendous force exists among us all! We don't have to be a member of the largest law firm in the community or the superintendent of a school or a county commissioner or a governor or president or a congressman to make a profound change in the lives of those who look at us.

While I was governor this was impressed on me very heavily by Dr. Norman Vincent Peale, who every year through his magazine [*Guideposts*] selects the outstanding church in the United States. The last year I was in office Dr. Peale and his organization recognized the church in Macon, Georgia, as the most outstanding church in the whole country. As governor I was invited to go and share the speaking platform with Dr. Peale. There were about six thousand people in the Macon Civic Auditorium and the members of the church sitting right in front of us. I knew what a tremendous speaker Dr. Peale was and how he could move an audience and I didn't want to be outdone, although I was. I worked hard on my speech.

Dr. Peale . . . made a speech about love and the different meanings of the word. The audience was gripped and moved. I made a good speech, following him, about the practical applications of Christianity in dealing with social problems.

The final thing on the program was for a member of the church to participate—the church that was chosen, by the way, by Dr. Peale was called The Church of Exceptionals. The church had thirty-five members, all retarded children, severely retarded, some of them, children of all ages.

There had been placed in front of the speaking platform a large white candle. A mongoloid woman, about forty-five, represented the congregation. She was to come and light the candle. She was helped up out of her chair. She was given a lighted flame, and she walked very slowly up in front of the audience while everyone in the room watched her closely. She was so retarded she had a hard time controlling her movements. She tried to light the candle and it wouldn't light. She couldn't bring the flame to where the wick was. And she tried again, and it wouldn't light. She looked around her shoulders at the other members of the little church, and in the whole six thousand persons, the congregation was very ill at ease and tense. She didn't know what to do. The pastor of the church, who was a layman, by the way, started to go forward and help her light the candle. She tried once more and the candle lit. I have never seen an audience moved as deeply as that large group was when she turned around and it saw the expression on her face because she had done all she could and she had done it well. And everybody knew what a difficulty it was for her to achieve that accomplishment. Much greater than my speech, much greater than Norman Vincent Peale's speech, that mongoloid woman lighting that candle for Christ still remains in every person's mind and heart that attended that service.

So we don't need, as Christian men, to analyze our own stature or status in the community. God looks at each one of us as individuals and wants us to demonstrate the life of

Christ. It's a sobering thought to know how people look at us and to know how far short we fall of that responsibility.

I don't know the answer to a lot of questions [we face] as individuals or as a nation. I see the injustice that exists in our criminal systems; I see the inequities that exist in opportunity among those who happen to be black or Spanish-speaking or whose parents were illiterate; I see the unfairness of our tax structures and the lack of opportunity to many young people to take whatever talent or ability and expand that talent through educational systems; and I see the shortcomings of our nation's government and political leaders in not measuring up to the standards or qualities or moral character of our people. These needs prey on my mind and they concern me much more deeply, I believe, because I, like you, have a perfect example in the life of Christ against which we're called upon to measure ourselves every moment of our existence.

I know that your denomination, as does mine, believes in a complete separation of church and state, but that doesn't mean we ought to have a different standard of ethics or morality or excellence or greatness or humility or brotherhood or compassion or love in public life from what we have in our private life.

The last day I was in Massachusetts with the Cuban Christian Eloy Cruz, we went by to see a young man whose wife had died. He was much better educated than the other Spanish-speaking people we had seen; he was a certified public accountant. His wife, who was only nineteen years old, had gone to a dentist to have a tooth extracted and because of a special mistake she had bled to death. They had a little baby. The young man was so wrought about his wife's death he tried to kill the little baby. He was kind of an outcast in the community. He had gone to a room in an apartment and he wouldn't speak to anyone. Eloy Cruz found out about it and went to see him.

The text of his talk was Revelations 3:20, "Behold, I stand at the door, and knock: if anyone hear my voice, and open the door, I will come in and sup with him, and he with me." Eloy Cruz told the young man that in spite of his sorrow and in spite of his loneliness Christ was available with all his love and all his protection and all his guidance and all his forgiveness for that young man who had tried to kill his own child.

It was such a moving experience for me that when we came out of the apartment onto the street—it was raining—I had tears running down my cheeks. It was the last day I would be with Eloy Cruz. In Spanish I asked him, "How is it that you, being such a tough he-man, are able to move and influence the lives of people as I have seen you do this week?" He was embarrassed because I had on nice clothes and I had a good automobile and so forth. He finally fumbled through a sentence in Spanish. He said, "*Nuestra Salvador*—Our Saviour—*tiene los manos*—has hands—*muy suaves*—that are very gentle or soft. *El puede hacer mucho*—He can do much—*conun hombre duro*—with a man who is hard. Our Saviour has hands that are very gentle. He can do much with a man who is hard."

Well, it's part of our problem as Christian laymen. We tend to be strong, stalwart, unemotional, proud, hard, when a truer demonstration of strength would be concern, compassion, love, emotion, sensitivity, humility—exactly the things Christ taught us about. I believe if we can demonstrate this kind of personal awareness of our own faith individually and as a group that we can provide that core strength and commitment and unchanging character that our nation searches for and perhaps the world itself.

There's no limit placed on us by God. The only limit we have is the voluntary self-imposed limit we put on ourselves when we refuse to accept the responsibilities offered to us, when we lower our standards in our public lives below those we know God demands. The Christian church doesn't change in its concepts, in its beliefs, in its hopes and ideals, and if we can retain our commitment to those principles and exemplify them as free men, then we can meet the expectations of our Lord.

To laymen of the Disciples of Christ, Lafayette, Indiana, June 18, 1976

DOWN TO WHERE THE SUFFERING IS

It would be difficult for you to know the impact of the African Methodist Church on my life. Unless you are familiar with my childhood in a little community named Archery, Georgia, you know we have about twenty-five black families and two white families. The most respected member of the community, the best educated member, the most famous member of the community, the most widely traveled member of the community, and the richest member in the community is Bishop William Johnson. He lives about a half mile west of where I lived. We looked on him with respect, friendship, admiration, brotherhood, and with love.

I have attended the tiny Archery AME church many times. When that great bishop would come from the Middle West, where I believe he had five states under his charge, he would invite our family and others to assemble once or twice a year. We would sit on the front lawn and listen to him preach. There was developed in our lives a feeling of mutuality, a common purpose, a common faith, a common future that still plays a part in my life.

This church of yours, the church of Christ, has provided a basis on which we could eliminate disharmony. It's taken a long time, but we've made a lot of progress in recent years. The single factor that can never be shaken and is bound up together was that mutual faith.

A lot of people in this country look on the South and say, "How could this have been done?" not recognizing the commonality of our suffering, of our deprivations, of our achievements, our hopes, our dreams, our aspirations. The church has let us look in the same direction as Christ looked, to those who need our ministrations the most.

I saw very early in my own life that those who make decisions, inventions, in the professions, education and government, are quite often the strong, the powerful, the influential, socially prominent, wealthy. When they make mistakes, their families are not the ones who suffer because they don't depend on welfare payments for food, clothing, for a place to sleep. When tax laws are grossly unfair, those politicians don't suffer because those tax laws are prepared by them for them and their friends. When unemployment rates climb—forty per cent of our young black men are out of work—their families don't stand in line for a job, and the intensity of the problem is not focused on those who quite often live in an ivory tower, in positions of prominence. They don't feel the need for change as do those who are poor, uneducated, unemployed, old, sick, black, or who don't speak good English.

The church has been the bridge that lets you move from ivory towers down to where the suffering is. . . .

The church is a good reminder that God is indeed with the lowly, the suffering, the deprived. If it hadn't been for the church that bridge would not have been there.

There's another bridge the church has provided—particularly your church. That is the one between black people and white people. There has been an unshakable commitment to human rights, civil rights, justice, concentrated here in Atlanta where the great colleges are. In the years when there was a lot of prejudice, hatred, lack of understanding, difficulty in communication, those great schools provided an unshakable commitment to what was right, what was decent, what was fair, what was just. . . .

There is a close correlation between worship services and correcting wrongs. That's what the Bible teaches, because Jesus Christ never hid himself seven days a week in the synagogue. He walked the streets. He touched blind eyes; He healed those who were crippled; He pointed out injustice. He brought about compassion and brotherhood and love. And he changed the lives of those who didn't go to church. And the more they were stricken with poverty or physical or mental affliction, the more time he spent with them.

This has been a role played by your great church in changing the times. We still have a long way to go.

When I was governor I visited all the prisons in the state to learn about those who were in the prisons and what could be done for them, their early release, better pardon and parole procedures, briefer, surer sentences, psychological counseling, more chaplain services, correction of alcoholism and drug addiction, to bring the prisoners back close to their families, let them out for good conduct on holidays so they could keep some contact with the outside world, and I got to know the characteristics of those who are in prison—a lot of old people, a lot of young people, a lot of black people, a lot of white people, a lot of well-educated people, a lot of retarded people—35 per cent of Georgia prisoners are mentally retarded—a lot of poor people, but not any rich people.

This doesn't mean that our criminal justice or court system has a conspiracy against poor people. We still have a long way to go in making sure that there is sure justice, there is sure equality of opportunity in this country under the law.

I don't mean to know all the answers. I've learned a lot and I'm still learning.

There is a need for some characteristic of our lives that never changes, because the family structure in a rural neighborhood like Archery, Georgia, is no longer there. When I was in trouble, when I was lonely, when I was doubtful, when I was fearful, my mother and father were always there; I could get to them. My brother and sisters were always there. You don't have that close family connection now that doesn't change and is always there. We didn't move very much. My ancestors were born in the 1700s and are buried right there in Plains, where I live, a few miles north of there. Now 20 per cent of all our people move every year. So we've got a lot of uncertainty in our lives. They're not held together as much as they were before. We need something in this country and in individual lives that never changes.

We've got that something that never changes—faith in God. That never changes and a search for truth, justice, equality, understanding, brotherhood, and love. The search is always there. A great theologian, Paul Tillich, said that religion is a search for the truth about man's existence, his relationship to God and his fellow man. When we quit searching, we lose our religion. When we think we've got it made and we're so good, when we keep forgetting about our own sins and those who need our ministry, our religion has no meaning.

This is true not only in the church, it's true in our nation. We've got a good country, the greatest on earth. Our system of government is the best on earth. Richard Nixon hasn't hurt our system of government; even Vietnam and Cambodia haven't hurt our system of government; or the CIA hasn't hurt our system of government. It's still clean and decent, the basis on which we can ask the difficult questions, correct our nation's shortcomings, but we've got to keep searching. We can't take anything for granted. We've got to be forceful. We can't lower our standards. So, in a lot of ways, our national life and our church life are parallel. They ought to be kept separate. I believe in the separation of church and state. That doesn't mean we ought to live two different lives, one as a politician and the other one as a churchman.

Now, a lot of people say that one person can't change the nation. That's not true. I remember in 1968 when the administrations of Lyndon Johnson and John Kennedy were over, and Richard Nixon came to the White House, the congress didn't change—it was still a Democratic congress—the country changed. It changed most for the people who need government the most. What people lost was hope.

I believe the time has come to restore that hope, not because it's me, but because this country suffered in the

last ten years. I believe there's an eagerness among our
people to search for a higher standard of ethics, morality,
excellence, greatness that can be derived from those who
have a knowledge of that higher standard.

We Christians have that knowledge; we have a perfect
example of what a person ought to be. We can't meet that
example, measure up to those standards, but we know
what it is. I want to see our country change for the better;
I want to see a government that's as good as our people
are; I want to see us take an individual standard in our
own lives which you and I have learned in church, sometimes the same church, and let us be a beacon light for the
redress of grievances, the end of discrimination, the grant-
ing of equality, the insurance of pure justice, the restoration of government, the building [in] this country of a
legitimate search for the finest possible aspects of human
beings.

We've made a lot of progress! We've got a long way to
go, but together, under God in this free nation, we're
going to get it.

> To ministers of the African Methodist Episcopal Church,
> Atlanta, Georgia, June 18, 1976

ON THE NEED FOR NATIONAL HUMILITY

ONE OF THE CHRISTIAN ATTRIBUTES I had in great abun-
dance—more than I do now—is humility. I had just been
defeated in my first campaign for Governor. The first
draft of my inaugural speech did not include the reference
to Micah's admonition about justice and mercy and humil-

ity. I had chosen instead II Chronicles 7:14: "If my people who are called by my name shall humble themselves and pray and seek my face and turn from their wicked ways, then will I hear from Heaven and forgive their sins and heal their land."

When my staff members read the first draft of my speech they rose up in opposition to that verse. The second time I had the same verse in it. And they came to me en masse and said, "The people will not understand that verse. It's as though you, being elected president, are condemning the other people of our country, putting yourself in the position of Solomon and saying that all Americans are wicked."

So, correctly or wrongly, I changed it to Micah. And I think this episode, which is true, is illustrative of the problem that we face. Sometimes we take for granted that an acknowledgment of sin, an acknowledgment of the need for humility permeates the consciousness of our people. But it doesn't. If we know we can have God's forgiveness as a person, I think, it makes it much easier for us to say, as a nation, "God, have mercy on me, a sinner," knowing that the only compensation for sin is condemnation. Then we just can admit an error or a weakness or hatred, or forgo pride. We as individuals—and we as a nation—insist that we are the strongest and the bravest and the wisest and the best. And in that attitude, we unconsciously, but in an all-pervasive way, cover up and fail to acknowledge our mistakes and in the process forgo an opportunity constantly to search for a better life or a better country.

Paul Tillich said that religion is a search for a closer relationship with God and our fellow man, and when we lose the inclination to search, to a great degree we lose our own religion. As those of us who are Christians know, the most constantly repeated admonition from Christ was against pride. Sometimes it's easier for us to be humble as individuals than it is for us to admit that our nation makes mistakes.

In effect, many of us worship our nation. We politicians, we leaders, in that sometimes excessive degree of patriotism, equate love of others with love of ourselves. We tend to say that, because I am a congressman, because I am a governor, because I am a senator, because I am a cabinet member, because I am president of the people, and because I love the people and because I represent them so well, I can justify their love myself. We tend to take on for ourselves the attributes of the people we represent. But when the disciples struggled among themselves for superiority in God's eyes, Jesus said, "Whosoever would be chief among you, let him be his servant" [paraphrase of Matthew 20:27]. And although we use the phrase, sometimes glibly, "public servant," it's hard for us to translate the concept of a President of the United States into genuine servant.

Another theologian I read very often, who could penetrate the pride of a nation in the most effective way in trying to analyze what democracy was, said a kind of prideful thing, but I think it brings to us a consciousness of our own capability. He said: "Man's capacity for justice makes democracy possible, but man's capacity for injustice makes democracy necessary."*

If we, as leaders of our nation, can search out and extract and discern and proclaim a new spirit, derived not from accumulated goodness or badness of people, which is only equal to individual goodness or badness—not even to

*See Reinhold Niebuhr, *The Children of Light and the Children of Darkness* (New York: Scribner's, 1944), p. viii.

the noble concept of our nation, which is superlative, without doubt, but from the ultimate source of goodness and kindness and humility and love, and that's from God—then we can indeed be good leaders and servants. We can indeed be strong enough and sure enough to admit our sinfulness and our mistakes. We can indeed be constantly searching for a way to rectify our errors and let our nation exemplify what we as individuals ought to be in the eyes of God. But that's a hard thing to do.

A book that made a great impression on me was *The Ugly American*, about people from our own country who, in a sense of unwarranted superiority, would travel around the world and despise others in an ostentatious way because they were not Americans.

But I've seen in my own travels a respect of us, a respect for our nation because of the same vision of our forefathers that has inspired us, but, at the same time, quite often a deep sense of disappointment that we don't live up to those original hopes and expectations and ideals.

Not too long ago I was in South America with my wife, and we had a chance to learn at first hand about the deep sense of religion there. We saw the impact of our own missionaries and when I visited the equivalent of their Speaker of the House, that evening in his home we spent time on our knees worshiping the same God. I preached one evening in a church in Rio de Janeiro, and a couple of years later my wife and I were in what's thought to be the tomb of Christ and a woman behind me looked at me in a strange way and said, "Don't I know you from somewhere?" I said, "No, ma'am, I don't think so." She said, "I think you preached in my husband's church in Rio." It was the wife of the pastor [of the Rio de Janeiro church].

A sense of communion we can have under God

throughout the world ought to convince us that we are not superior, that we ought constantly to search out national and individual consciousness and strive to be better, which doesn't mean more powerful and autocratic, but more filled with love and understanding and compassion and humaneness and humility. . . .

A search for peace, I believe, can only be successful if we recognize the commonality of the aspirations of human beings throughout the world and if we remember that cumulative humility ought never to be equated to dominant national pride.

National Prayer Breakfast, Washington, D.C., January 27, 1977

SERVANTS OF GOD

. . . To ME, God is real. To me, the relationship with God is a very personal thing. God is ever-present in my life, sustains me when I am weak, gives me guidance when I turn to Him, and provides for me, as a Christian, the life of Christ—a perfect example to emulate in my experiences with other human beings.

My wife and I worship together every night, and often during the day I turn to God in a quiet and personal way.

A few months back, the words "born again" [John 3:3] were vividly impressed on the consciousness of many Americans who were not familiar with their meaning. They've been used in many headlines and on the front covers of many magazines. But for those of us who share the Christian faith, the words "born again" have a very simple meaning: that through a personal experience, we recommit our lives as humble children of God, which makes us in the realest possible sense brothers and sisters of one another. Families are bound by the closest possible ties.

I noticed a small news item this morning that I was chosen "Lover of the Year." It concerned me very much until I read on and found that it was because my wife and I have been in love for more than thirty-one years, and that the exemplification of a close family life is the best expression of love.

But for a member of Congress, for a governor, for an executive officer who cares for hundreds of thousands of veterans of war, for the commanding general of the United States Marines, for foreign dignitaries, and for a president, the word "family" has a broader meaning—the family of all human beings and how we might alleviate world tensions and hatred and misunderstandings and death and suffering and loneliness and alienation through a common understanding and a common purpose, and sometimes even a common belief.

A few weeks ago I was in India. As part of my preparation for meeting with Indian leaders, I read the *Bhagavad-Gita* and later visited the site where Mahatma Gandhi's body was cremated and thought about his simple, deeply committed life, his knowledge of Christianity and Judaism, his worship of God, the simplicity and humility and sensitivity of his life. And I felt a kinship with him and a kinship of the Indian leaders who have not always been our friends in recent years. And as I talked to Prime Minister Desai, this was a common thread that ran through the conversation between us—how we shared something.

The Preaching Mission

Last year at a relatively small supper at the White
House, Crown Prince Fahd from Saudi Arabia, when
asked a question by a member of the group, a member of
Congress—how would Saudi Arabia with its tremendous
growing wealth deal with the needs of its own people and
hold together as a community—gave one of the most elo-
quent impromptu speeches I have ever heard about how
common religious faith, and their responsibility to hold
together the interest in the holy places of Islam, gave him
confidence in the future and guidance on how his own
life should be expended in the services of others.

I met with Prime Minister Begin twice during this past
year and hope to see him again soon when he comes to our
country. I like him, admire him, and respect him, because
throughout his conversations with me in the quiet, lonely,
private times together, and even when he talks with others
in a larger group, there is a fervor of a deeply committed
religious man who again worships the same God I do, and
you do. I felt an instant friendship with President Sadat.
And in his messages to me and in my talks to him, he
never fails to point out that the Egyptians and the Jews are
sons of Abraham, worship the same God, share a common
heritage and a common faith, and that this is a transcendent thing, quite often forgotten, but still there; that it
doesn't change.

And in our own search for peace and goodwill, in spite
of setbacks and criticisms and sometimes the undertaking
of tasks that are not easily performed, I have a sense of
confidence that if we emphasize and reinforce those ties of
mutual faith and our subservience and humility before
God and an acquiescence in His deeply sought guidance,
that we can prevail.

The leaders of our nation look with a great deal of con-

[249]

cern over past experiences when kings and princesses had tied themselves to God, to the church, sometimes even in an exalted position relative to God, and had cloaked maladministration and injustice in the protection of the church. So in our Constitution, we carefully prescribed that there should be no establishment of religion in this country.

So we worship freely. But that does not mean that leaders of our nation and the people of our nation are not called upon to worship, because those who wrote the Declaration of Independence and the Bill of Rights and our Constitution did it under the aegis of, the guidance of, and with full belief in God.

In our rapidly changing world, we need to cling to things that don't change, to truth and justice, to fairness, to brotherhood, to love and to faith. And through prayer, I believe that we can find those things. I don't think that's overly optimistic. And when Judge Sirica [U.S. District Judge, John J. Sirica, who presided over most Watergate cases], one of the great men of all times in our country, referred to Solomon, I thought about the time described in the First Book of Kings . . . when God said to Solomon, "What do you want from me?" And Solomon said, "Give Thy servant an understanding mind to govern your people, that I might discern between good and evil." And God said, "That's such a fine prayer that I will not only grant you wisdom, but I will grant you the other blessings of life as well" [paraphrase of I Kings 3:15–17].

Almost everyone in this room is a leader, trusted by others, looked up to by others, respected by others, influential among others. And I pray that that doesn't give us a sense of pride or exaltation or a sense of self-satisfaction, but that it gives us a sense of humility and that we turn to

God through prayer so that we might better serve those who have placed their faith in us as we place our faith in God.

National Prayer Breakfast, Washington, D.C., February 2, 1978

THE INWARD AND OUTWARD JOURNEY

I WOULD LIKE TO TALK TO YOU from the perspective of a president. I have been in office now not quite a year and a half, and I have seen very clearly that government touches every life and that what the American government does touches people in every other nation because of the power, the strength, the influence, the wealth of our country.

This puts a tremendous responsibility on me as a public official, but it also puts a tremendous responsibility on you, every one of you, as American citizens, because in a free society like our own, we are not only blessed with a chance to grow, to learn, to stretch our hearts and minds in total freedom, but our religious convictions teach us how that freedom might be used and the limits of it as we serve others.

And in a democracy we know that we share and control the government to the extent that we are willing to participate and contribute our influence. So, in effect, as Americans, as Christians, we not only shape our own lives and set an example for our neighbors immediately around us, but we also shape what our country is and what it hopes to be in the future, therefore, influencing people throughout the world.

As president, I still look on government in a personal way, which is a surprise to some people. Last year I got a letter from a child who said, "Now that you have been in office for six months or so, would you rather be President or a real person?"

That question has preyed on my mind. In a modern, fast-changing technical world, we tend to be dehumanized, stamped out in a pattern. Individual traits that give us a uniqueness in God's world tend to be ironed out and smoothed over. This creates conflicts in us because there is a difference between our attitude toward our private inward life and our public outward life, no matter how broad the scope of our participation might be in public affairs.

I remember in Plains, Georgia, our house was only about thirty, forty yards from the railroad track. And as a tiny boy I used to stand there and watch those tremendous steam engines go by with the big yellow wheels and I would watch the connecting rods pushing forward, pulling back, pushing forward, pulling back, and the wheel went around and the train went forward. And I couldn't understand it for a long time, but now I see very clearly that, unless a connecting rod went forward and back, the wheel could not have continued to turn and the train could not have made any progress.

Well, we as Baptists, as Christians, as Americans, are trying to make progress. The bold mission effort is a new ideal, a new program, a new commitment, a new concept which lets us as a denomination spread our influence in a benevolent way much more rapidly, much more broadly, than we had contemplated a few years ago.

I have noticed this convention has concentrated on how we might use our position in life to greater influence in the service of God. But quite often we are much more interested in using our influence for ourselves, for material benefit, for stature, for a good reputation, for influence, even to win in the competition of life more than we were or are or possibly will be in God's service.

When I was a naval officer, a scientist, a businessman, I was intensely committed to doing well. I worked many hours every day. I thought at night about how I might do better. When I was a candidate for public office, particularly the last campaign I ran, I gave a hundred percent of everything in me to win, to let the American people know the good side of my character, perhaps to conceal my defects, to let them realize how badly I wanted to serve.

I didn't waste any time and neither did my family, and neither did many friends. But I have to stand here and confess to you that I have never given that much of a sustained commitment to serving God.

But this is not an inherent limit on human beings just because I or perhaps some of you are guilty of that misapplication of priorities, because there have been many times in the past when individual people adopted in their own lives a bold mission and not only changed their own lives, but were able to use their lives in a way that carried on through history.

Abraham Lincoln, Mahatma Gandhi, Martin Luther King, Jr. were people who used their influence in political ways to correct wrongs, to open up new possibilities for other people to expand their hearts, to expand their minds, to live better lives.

They lost their lives through violence in this carrying out of a bold mission for themselves. In our own denomination, we have seen the same thing. [Others] gave their lives quite often unrecognized, unappreciated while they were alive, but we know that these transformed the concept of Christian mission because they persevered. They had journeys, a journey inward, a journey outward; inward to find peace of one's spirit, to struggle with doubt, to struggle with fear, to lay one's fears on God, to build up strength, to turn outward for an expanded life, a more fruitful life to benefit others.

These two are linked, sometimes shifting from one to another in a matter of a second or two. Sometimes long periods of time are required to shift from an inner finding of one's self to the use of one's self for others. Sometimes Baptists have been too inclined to turn inwardly and to stay that way, within a person, within a home, within a church. That can be a defect; it is not necessarily good for us to deny, because of a search for inner peace, the rest of the world.

As we know ourselves, we know God better. We are able to face fears leading to a full life.

Some of us in public service turn to politics, to public service on a full-time basis. This is not contrary to Christian beliefs. Isaiah and Jeremiah pronounced God's judgment in the very center of political power. So no conflict prevents bringing one's personal religious life together with the political arena. There is a danger, obviously, of conflict, of collusion—Baptists are very much aware of that. Thomas Jefferson said that he was fearful that the church might influence the state to take away human liberty. Roger Williams, who created the first Baptist church in our country, was afraid that the church might be corrupted by the state. These concerns led to the First Amendment, which prohibits the establishment of any official state church, and on the other hand, in the same sentence, prohibits the passing of any laws that might interfere with religious freedom.

Separation is specified in the law, but, for a religious person, there is nothing wrong with bringing these two together. You can't divorce religious beliefs from public service. And at the same time, of course, in public office you cannot impose your own religious beliefs on others.

I have never detected or experienced any conflict between God's will and my political duty. It is obvious that when I violate one at the same time I violate the other. Politics is not unsavory. It is not degrading. It is not something of which we need to be ashamed.

In my acceptance speech at the Democratic Convention almost two years ago, I said that I wanted an opportunity to translate, aggressively translate, love into simple justice. Well, that is my chance as one individual, no better than you, to adopt a bold mission.

All of us, in our own special way, are influential. And we know that Christ says that unto whosoever much is given, much will be required, and to whom men commit much, they will demand more [Luke 12:48]. Too many of us, as Americans, as Christians, are derelict in the duty of [using] our influence, our power, our wealth, our free time, and dealing with those issues that still remain as a great challenge to us all. We tend to ignore the fact that challenges are there.

I will just give you one example: human rights. More than a century ago, our ancestors, yours and mine, were in the forefront of those dedicated to the preservation of slavery. More recently, you and I were not in the forefront of those dedicated to eliminating segregation, racial discrimination among our own neighborhood, friends.

Particularly in the South, we have spoken on this basic issue with a voice that is too timid.

[We] as individuals [must] reach out in our own community, in our nation, around the world, to detect and to destroy those elements of life which still interfere with the realization of those hopes and dreams of people who are afflicted and deprived. I hope that our country never again turns its back because of convenience or embarrassment as we did when millions of Jews lost their lives in the Holocaust during the Second World War. . . . [In] my office at the White House, I have to deal with many domestic problems, many international problems: peace, freedom, nuclear explosives, the sale of weapons, terrorism, rapidly expanding populations without food. But this is more than a list of political problems. These are also for you and me moral problems because they violate the very precepts of God in which we believe. Reinhold Niebuhr, in his book *Moral Man and Immoral Society,** pointed out the difference between a society and people: The expectations and demands on a person are a much higher standard. A person should have as a goal complete *agape*—love. The most we can accept or expect from a society is to institute simple justice.

Leaders have to be careful not to be too timid. Sometimes we are reluctant to deal with a complicated issue or a contemptuous issue; controversy scares us. . . . No one likes to fail, because you bring upon yourself a bad reputation, derision, scorn, embarrassment. And sometimes the best way to avoid failure is not to try very hard, not to be in the center of a noble effort or to quit soon enough so you will not be associated in the end with disappointment.

Moral Man and Immoral Society: A Study in Ethics and Politics (New York: Scribner's, 1932).

I want our country to be pre-eminent in many ways, not just pre-eminent in military might, but pre-eminent in those characteristics of which we can all be proud after careful scrutiny. I want our country to be strong enough . . . so we never have to prove we are strong. A person who is strong and knows it can then afford not to prove it and can be gentle and fair, and patient and understanding and generous. . . .

We know that our security is bound up with that of others. We cannot any more depend upon the isolation of friendly neighbors and deep oceans. And we cannot any more depend upon a dominant military force with a monopoly on nuclear weapons. So we cannot ignore others because we are isolated. We cannot dominate others any more because we are strong. We have a new opportunity, a new responsibility. And how we handle this changing factor in an international world will be a measure of our emotional and our spiritual maturity.

Power, wealth, is not enough. We must be willing and able to analyze our own faults. And I think anyone knows that the character of American life has been tested and the fabric held together as we experienced the Vietnam war, the Watergate disgraces, the revelations about the CIA. Our country was tested, and because our people had an inner strength our country has not been permanently damaged; my judgment is that it is now stronger than ever.

A country will have authority and influence because of moral factors, not military factors, because it can be humble and not blatant and arrogant, because our people and our country want to serve others and not dominate others. [If we have] conflict with God, we have conflict with our fellow human beings. And a nation without morality will soon lose its influence around the world. A nation, like a person, has to be continually on an inward journey and an outward journey, and we grow stronger in the process. There is a relationship between personal leadership and a people.

Moses demonstrated this, as you know, when God called to him to lead the Israelites out of Egypt. He was not ready to assume that responsibility until he had spent forty years tending sheep, acquiring a family, discussing the problems with his father-in-law, Jethro. And he finally was able, reluctantly, to turn to God for help and support and a kind of a partnership, and then he was able to work with and sometimes against the people of Israel as they made their long, tortuous journey. [See Exodus 3.]

The goals of a person or a denomination or a country are all remarkably the same: a desire for peace, a need for humility, for examining one's faults and turning away from them; a commitment to human rights, in the broadest sense of the word, based on a moral society concerned with the alleviation of suffering because of deprivation or hatred or hunger or physical affliction. And a willingness, even an eagerness, to share one's ideals, one's faith, with others; to translate love in a person into justice.

Thomas Jefferson, as he considered what the emblem of our nation ought to be, the seal of the United States, suggested that it be a picture of the people of Israel following a cloud and a column of fire, because he saw this inner journey and the outward journey interrelated, and visualized, although he was not a very deeply religious man on the outside, that dependence on God was good for his new nation that he loved.

The great outward journey of the Israelites, of our own nation, was based on an inward journey where peace was derived from an inner strength and an awareness of the will of God and a willingness to carry this will out.

Southern Baptist Brotherhood Commission, Atlanta, Georgia, June 16, 1978

Scripture Index

Subject Index

abortion, 102-103, 111
adultery, 13, 70, 102
African Methodist Church, 238, 239
anti-Christ, 166-167, 177
anxiety:
  in Christian life, 215-216
  creativity of, 214-224
  death and, 217
  definition of, 216
  goals and, 215
  as good, 69-70, 216
  Niebuhr on, 214-215
  present as age of, 222-223
  substitution vs. change of, 216
  Tillich on, 214
  types of, 216-217
apocalyptic, 155
Archery, Ga., 238, 241
Assad, Hafiz, 134
assassination, 64

baptism, 159
Baptists, 109, 119, 204, 254
  believers as saints among, 163

doctrine and, 145, 179-180, 185, 186
  as elite, 168-169, 187
  faith of, 145
  obligations of, 118-119
Barnabas, 160-161
barriers:
  breaking down of, 193-205
  churches as, 92, 190-191
  as self-built, 205
  types of, 202-203
Begin, Menachem, 134, 135, 136, 137,
  249
Bhagavad-Gita, 62, 248
Bible:
  acceptance of, 16
  Christian doctrine's source in, 180
  civil law and, 70-71
  "holiness code" in, 26-27
  human rights in, 29-30
  injunction of peace in, 132-138
  love in, 22-24
  power as servanthood in, 25-27
  resurrection in, 209, 217
  women in, 16-18, 197-204, 208-210,
  213, 214

Bill of Rights, 250
 values advocated in, 90
blacks:
 as Carter audience, 30-31
 church and, 144, 161, 240
 civil rights and, 125, 202
 Plains Baptist Church and, 27-29
 Samaritans as, 197
 simple justice and, 89
 Truman and, 127
"born again," 2, 3-4, 110
 meaning of, 9-10, 247-248
Buber, Martin, 191
Burns, Arthur F., 193
Burns, George, 221

Caiaphas, 176-178
caring, 58
Carter, Jimmy:
 commitment to Christ of, 4, 11, 14
 farm background of, 226-227
 interpreting faith of, 9-22
 marriage and family life of, 11, 18-20
 as missionary, 6-7, 21-22, 176, 196,
  231-233
 Plains Baptist Church and, 19-20,
  27-29, 49-50, 52-54
 Playboy interview and, 13-14
 politics linked to religion by, 5,
  14-15, 23-32
 power as servanthood for, 25-29
 religious background of, 4-9,
  230-233, 238
 spiritual crisis of, 5-6, 7-8
 themes in prayers and teachings of,
  11
 theologians' influence on, 16
Christ:
 God's relation to, 175, 176, 181
 human experience of, 203-204
 manifestation of, 14
 meaning of, 4, 7, 8, 16, 116
 miracles of, 211, 220
 as model, 122-123, 223, 247
 as national example, 193
 partnerships with, 219

 as perfect image of God, 191
 resurrection of, 209, 217
 second coming of, 153-156
 as servant, 170
 union with, 183, 185
 virgin birth of, 164
Christian doctrine, 144-145
 Baptists and, 145, 179-180, 185, 186
 Bible as source of, 180
 church role in, 144, 186
 false, 145, 163-165, 179-180, 182-185
 Paul on, 179-180, 182-184
 testing of, 166, 167
 way of life and, 186
Christianity:
 abandoned values of, 193
 common purposes in, 119
 conflicts in, 156-162, 164-166
 crucial teaching in, 164-165, 207-208
 in daily life, 228
 dual relationship in, 181
 logic vs. faith in, 164-168
 magnification of self through, 114
 miraculous transformations as defined in, 9-10
 other religions compared with,
  180-181
 paradox in, 13, 181
 personal religion vs. world in, 22-25
 radical concepts in, 17, 25, 31
 second-class citizenship absent in, 84
 as simple faith, 165
 standards in, 223-224
 uniqueness of, 180
Christmas, meaning of, 149, 205
churches:
 as anti-Christ, 177
 as barrier to justice, 92
 as bridge, 240
 establishment of, 143-144
 God's kingdom and, 176-178
 government and, 124
 mission of, 143-144
 mutual admiration society in, 168
 purpose of, 144, 186
 standards of, 192

Messiah:
Jewish view of, 200
Samaritan view of, 200-201
Middle east:
religious commitment as basis for
peace in, 15, 134, 135, 137
Sadat-Begin peace meeting on,
133-136
missionaries and missions, 6-7, 21-22,
252, 254
commitment and, 145-147
God's kingdom expanded by, 178
Moses, 129, 200, 258

national security, 257
nations:
as "afflicted," 15
morality of, 257-259
worship of, 245-246
news media, Carter's religious faith
and, 2-3, 12, 14, 16-18, 117
Niebuhr, Reinhold, 97, 256
on anxiety, 214-215
on democracy, 245
on law, 107
on politics and justice, 25, 90, 162
Nixon, Richard, 242
Noah, 155
nonviolence, 95-96

obedience, Christian love and, 218,
221, 223
Ottenad, Tom, 74

pain, sharing of, 82
paraclete, defined, 219
patience, need for, 38
Paul, Apostle, 144, 160-162
on doctrine, 179-180, 182-184
on eternal life, 65, 213
as great teacher, 182
on resurrection, 217
peace, inner, 56-60, 222-224
peace, international, 247
Biblical injunction of, 132-138
Old Testament vision of, 94-95

peacemakers, 138
Peale, Norman Vincent, 234-235
permanence, 229
need for, 241-242, 250
Peter, Apostle, 157-161
church established by, 143
as model for human frailty, 70,
159-160
Plains, Ga., 4, 226-227, 241, 252
Plains Baptist Church, 19-20, 27-29,
49-50, 52-54
politics:
as ministry, 5
missionaries and, 22
religion linked to, 5, 14-15, 23-32
Powell, Jody, 2
power:
abuse of, 25-26
as servanthood, 25-27, 122-131
as shaper of law, 97, 239
prayer, 39-55
for Christian love, 51-52
confession through, 44
for daily discipline, 48
in daily life, 40-42, 48
for guidance, 12, 21, 42-43, 44-45
for healing, 49-50
for intimacy with Christ, 47-48
for meaningful life, 39, 92-93
for open heart and mind, 45-47
as personal and voluntary, 142
petitionary, 42-44
for reconciliation and peace, 49-50,
52-54, 134-136
of rededication, 49
self-realization through, 42
social support with, 45, 129
for unity through love of God, 55
preaching:
on inward and outward journey,
251-259
on national humility, 243-247
on servants of God, 247-251
on standards, 226-238
on suffering, 238-243
preaching mission, 225-238
pressure, yielding to, 70

Subject Index

pride, 169, 176, 245
 hazards of, 175, 176, 228, 247
 temptation and, 72-73
 as worst sin, 13, 15, 228
Primitive Baptist Church, 169-170
prisons, reforms in, 240-241
progress, through missions, 252
public servants. *See* servants, public
public service, faith and, 114-121, 254, 255

racial discrimination, 89, 255
 in Bible, 197
 King and, 95-96
reconciliation through love, 80-82
religion:
 communication and common purpose in, 136
 false definitions of, 191
 history influenced by, 133-134
 institutional vs. natural, 195-196
 joy in, 16
 purpose of, 149
 as search, 16, 77, 171, 233-234, 242, 244
repentance:
 injury and, 80-82
 as personal, 120-121
resources, natural, 132-133
responsibility:
 of Americans, 251, 255
 fallibility of leader and, 128-129
 of private citizens, 127-128
Roosevelt, Theodore, 102
ruthlessness, 73-75

Saadi, 82
sacrifice, need for, 38
Sadat, Anwar el-, 134, 135, 136, 137, 249
salvation, 162
 faith and, 178-187
Samaria, 196-197
Samaritans, 197-202
 Jews and, 197
 Messiah as viewed by, 200-201
 as racial outcasts, 197

Samaritan woman, 197-204
Saudi Arabia, 249
second coming, 153-156
segregation, 27-29
self-confidence, 16, 57-58
self-reliance, criticism of, 191-192
self-satisfaction, relationship with God and, 16, 37, 77, 223
servants:
 attitude of, 122-123
 of God, 247-251
 planners as, 122
 power as, 25-29
servants, public:
 as examples, 124-127
 president as, 123, 245
 selection of, 100
 youth and, 125-127
sin, 13, 116
 admission of, 175-176
 Humphrey and, 71-72
 judgment and, 70-71
Sirica, John J., 250
Solomon, on servants, 250
sorrow, sharing of, 82
South America, religion in, 246
Southern Baptist Convention, truck driver at, 194-195
standards, in Christianity, 223-224, 226-238, 243
Stapleton, Ruth Carter, 7-8, 11-12, 27
stewardship, 185
 as essence of Christian doctrine, 182
success, self-satisfaction and, 77-78, 223
suffering, 238-243
Sychar, 197, 198, 201
symbolism:
 of cross, 188
 importance of, 189
 of water, 91-92, 198-200, 203
 see also images, graven

teachers, false, 163-165, 167
teachings, 153-224
 on admission of sin, 175-176
 on anxiety, 214-224